Karl Marx

Early Writings

In the same series:

Karl Marx: Selected Writings in Sociology
and Social Philosophy, translated by
T. B. Bottomore edited by Mr. Bottomore and
Maximilien Rubel. Foreword by Erich Fromm

KARL MARX

EARLY WRITINGS

TRANSLATED AND EDITED BY
T. B. BOTTOMORE

FOREWORD BY ERICH FROMM

McGRAW-HILL BOOK COMPANY
NEW YORK   TORONTO   LONDON

© T. B. Bottomore, 1963
Foreword by Erich Fromm:
Copyright © 1964 by Erich Fromm
All Rights Reserved
First McGraw-Hill Edition, 1964

Printed in the United States of America

Library of Congress Catalog Card Number 64-21251

121314151617 MUMU 765432

ISBN 07-040671-5

CONTENTS

FOREWORD

Few authors have had the fate of being misunderstood and
distorted as Marx has been. Few authors, also, have been so
often quoted and so little read. Yet we can see in the last few
years a definite turn in this situation. After Marx had been
looked upon as a devil by the antisocialist side, and as an idol
—quoted and worshiped, but not understood—by the Soviet
side, a new wave of interest and research in Marxist theory is
sweeping Europe and America. Marx has truly been rediscov-
ered, and one does not go too far in saying that we are wit-
nessing the beginning of a renaissance of Marxist thought.

The effect of this renaissance is, first of all, to cease making
a dead saint of Marx and to restore him to the position of a
living thinker. Secondly, it tends to cease cutting Marx into
two parts: the "young Marx," still an idealist and concerned
with such concepts as the essence of man, and the "mature
Marx," mainly or exclusively interested in economics, according
to whom socialism (or communism) is defined as a system in
which the means of production are in the hands of the state
or the working class. It is true that Marx changed his terminology; thus, for instance, he stopped using the term "the essence
of man"; but he did not fundamentally change the substance
of his thought about man's nature. This holds specifically true
for the concept of alienation, which is the key concept in the
Economic and Philosophical Manuscripts, and which Marx re-
tained until the end of his life. Nothing could demonstrate this
better than comparing a sentence written by the young Marx
with a paragraph from his last work, the third volume of
Capital. In the *German Ideology,* Marx wrote: "Man's own
deed becomes an alien power opposed to him, which enslaves
him instead of being controlled by him." And "This crystalliza-
tion of social activity, this consolidation of what we ourselves

produce into an objective power above us, growing out of our control, thwarting our expectations, bringing to naught our calculations, is one of the chief factors in historical development up till now." At the end of *Capital,* volume III, Marx wrote:

The realm of freedom only begins, in fact, where that labour which is determined by need and external purposes, ceases; it is therefore, by its very nature, outside the sphere of material production proper. Just as the savage must wrestle with Nature in order to satisfy his wants, to maintain and reproduce his life, so also must civilized man, and he must do it in all forms of society and under any possible mode of production. With his development the realm of natural necessity expands, because his wants increase, but at the same time the forces of production, by which these wants are justified, also increase. Freedom in this field cannot consist of anything else but the fact that socialized mankind, the associated producers, regulate their interchange with Nature rationally, bring it under their common control, instead of being ruled by it as by some blind power, and accomplish their task with the least expenditure of energy and under such conditions as are proper and worthy for human beings. Nevertheless, this always remains a realm of necessity. Beyond it begins that development of human potentiality for its own sake, the true realm of freedom, which however, can only flourish upon that realm of necessity as its basis. The shortening of the working day is its fundamental prerequisite.

This paragraph represents the quintessence of Marx's thought: man can never transcend the realm of necessity, which is that of material production. But he can achieve an optimum of freedom even in this realm of necessity by the fact that "the associated producers regulate their interchange with Nature rationally, bring it under their common control, instead of being ruled by it as by some blind power. . . ." Here we find the same concept of alienation and de-alienation as in the early writings. In the following sentence Marx says that such a social order is the basis for the "development of human potentiality for its own sake, the true realm of freedom." Marx, at the end of his life, could not have expressed more clearly the goals and values which inspired him from the days of his youth, and thus confirmed the unity of his work against all later attempts at dividing and distorting it.

Marx was a humanist, for whom man's freedom, dignity, and activity were the basic premises of the "good society." As a humanist he believed in the unity of all men, and in man's capacity to find a new harmony with man and with nature. But Marx, while sharing the aims of Spinoza and Goethe, added a new dimension to humanism. He recognized that education alone will not transform man. He saw that man is to a large extent determined by his practice of life, and that if man wants to change he has to change the very circumstances which imprison him. In capitalism, so Marx thought, man is made to be a person who *has* much, who *uses* much, but who *is* little. Hence, in order to create the basis for the free development of man's potentialities, mankind must do away with a social-economic structure which by its very nature feeds man's greed and possessiveness. Socialization and planning are *means* to this end, but not an end in themselves. Socialism, if it is limited to the sphere of economics, is not humanism; it is not socialism.

These are the premises of those who participate in the renaissance of Marxism today. The representatives of this humanist socialism can be found in Great Britain, the United States, France, West Germany, Italy, Africa, India, Australia, Japan, and particularly the small socialist states: Yugoslavia, Poland, Czechoslovakia, and Hungary. It is an amazing fact that today there is more active Marx scholarship and study going on in the world than perhaps at any time since Marx's death.[1]

While we stress the differences between Marxist and non-

---

[1] Evidence of this renaissance is to be found in a symposium on socialist humanism, edited by Erich Fromm, to be published by Doubleday & Company, Inc.

Marxist humanists, we must realize that Marx's humanism is today part of a renaissance of humanism which is to be found among Catholics and Protestants as well as among nonreligious scientists and philosophers. This new humanism has arisen as a reaction to the double threat which menaces mankind today: the threat of nuclear war and the destruction of all life, or "at best" of civilization as we know it, and the threat of complete alienation in which man, in producing and serving things, transforms himself into a thing. Contemporary humanism, like Renaissance humanism, is an expression of protest against the danger of dehumanization. But it is more than a protest; it is the expression of faith in man's having the alternative to choose a full life instead of destruction, and in his capacity to make the right choice if only he is aware of the underlying forces inside himself and within society.

The works of Marx collected in this volume are among the most important of his humanist writings. Without understanding them one can hardly understand Marx's later writings, just as the earlier ones can hardly be understood without a knowledge of the later works.

A few comments on the three works published here may assist the reader in understanding them. The paper "On the Jewish Question" is one of the most brilliant of Marx's treatises, analysing the nature of bourgeois society and discussing the difference between political emancipation and human emancipation. It is one of the symptoms showing to what degree the falsification of Marx can go that some years ago a reputable publishing house in the United States published this work (in a bad and distorted translation) under the title "A World without Jews" (a title never thought of by Marx) and advertised the book with statements about Marx's being an anti-Semite and responsible for Hitler's and Stalin's anti-Semitism. Anyone familiar with Marx's views and personal life will realize the absurdity of this construction. He knows furthermore that Marx was a true internationalist who had no preference for any nation, and who was critical of all, never respecting the taboos of national feeling. While in this paper he said some harsh (and in my opinion not always correct) words about what he thought was the Jewish religion, he said equally harsh words about the British shopkeepers, the German philosophers, and the Russians. To designate Marx as an anti-Semite is nothing but cold-war propaganda; it is most fortunate that this propaganda will be counteracted by the excellent and honest translation offered in this collection.

In "The Critique of Hegel's Philosophy of Right" another widespread error is corrected: the error that Marx was against the "spiritual" and for the "material"; that his criticism of religion was motivated by this "materialism." The opposite is true. Marx saw in religion "the illusory happiness" of men, and in the abolition of religion a "demand for their real happiness." "The call to abandon their illusions," he wrote, "is a call to *abandon a condition which requires illusions.*" Marx's criticism of religion was not based on the idea that man should enjoy material satisfactions instead of spiritual ones. He maintained that religion failed in its function and gave man illusions, rather than enabling him "to pluck the living flower." "The criticism of religion disillusions man, so that he will think, act, and fashion his reality as a man who has lost his illusions and regained his reason; so that he will revolve about himself as his own true sun. Religion is only the illusory sun about which man revolves so long as he does not revolve about himself."

Marx's aim is the *dis*-illusioned, independent man, not the brainwashed object of manipulation. The man "who revolves about himself" is not a narcissistic or an egoistic man, but a free man who owes his existence to himself. This man is not only free *from* chains, but free *to be* himself, to be authentically related to his fellow man and to nature. Marx's free man is an *active* and *productive* man. Nowhere has Marx expressed this more beautifully than in his discussion of money in the third of the *Economic and Philosophical Manuscripts:*

"Let us assume *man* to be *man,* and his relation to the world to be a human one. Then love only can be exchanged for love, trust for trust, etc. If you wish to enjoy art you must be an artistically cultivated person; if you wish to influence other people you must be a person who really has a stimulating and encouraging effect upon others. Every one of your relations to man and to nature must be a *specific expression,* corresponding to the object of your will, of your *real individual* life. If you love without evoking love in return, i.e. if you are not able, by the *manifestation* of yourself as a loving person, to make yourself a *beloved person,* then your love is impotent and a misfortune."

Erich Fromm
May 1964

INTRODUCTION

In an earlier book [1] Dr. Rubel and I presented a selection of texts which was intended to show the nature of Marx's sociological thought and its relevance to modern sociology. Many of the texts, and especially those of the period 1843–5, were little known in the English-speaking countries.[2] Since then, Marx's early writings have been much discussed, but they are still not easily accessible in satisfactory English translations. In the present volume, therefore, I have provided translations of three of the most important of these early works: the two essays, " On the Jewish Question " and " Contribution to the Critique of Hegel's Philosophy of Right. Introduction," which were first published in the *Deutsch-Französische Jahrbücher* (1844); and the " Economic and Philosophical Manuscripts " (1844).[3]

The wider knowledge of Marx's early writings has played an important part, alongside the social and political changes in both Western and Eastern societies, in bringing about a reconsideration of his social theories. These writings have been interpreted in a number of different ways. In the first place, they have been regarded as expounding a moral doctrine which remained the basis of all Marx's intellectual and political activity even though it was less explicitly stated in his later writings.[4] This doctrine, which Marx calls

---

[1] T. B. BOTTOMORE and MAXIMILIEN RUBEL, *Karl Marx: Selected Writings in Sociology and Social Philosophy*, London, 1956, 2nd impression, 1961.

[2] Marx's early writings were first comprehensively discussed, in English, in H. P. ADAMS, *Karl Marx in his Earlier Writings*, London, 1940. This interesting book does not, however, contain many direct translations from the texts.

[3] Further notes on the texts and translations are given later in this Introduction. A part of my translation of the " Economic and Philosophical Manuscripts " has been published in ERICH FROMM, *Marx's Concept of Man*, New York, 1961.

[4] *See* the illuminating discussion in ERICH FROMM, op. cit. The " humanism " of the young Marx has provided much support for the intellectual opposition to bureaucratic and police rule in the Communist countries; for example

" humanism," formulates the ideal of a community of men who are able to develop freely, and in harmony with each other, all their personal qualities.   Marx takes for granted the creed of the Enlightenment—the innate goodness of man, human perfectibility, the power of human reason [1]—but he expresses it in a new form which is influenced by the development of industrial capitalism and of the new science of political economy.   Marx's ideal is the *productive* man, contrasted with the *acquisitive* man.[2]   For this conception Marx is also indebted to Hegel, as he himself acknowledges: " The outstanding achievement of Hegel's *Phenomenology* . . . is, first, that Hegel grasps the nature of *labour*, and conceives of objective man . . . as the result of his *own labour*." [3]   Moreover, Marx goes on to describe the actual condition of man in industrial society by the Hegelian term " alienation."   Man is alienated in two senses: first, the vast majority of men (and perhaps all men) have lost control of the products of their own activity, which now confront them as inhuman ruling powers;   secondly, in the process of work itself most men are not productive in the sense of exercising freely their natural powers, but are constrained to perform uninteresting and degrading tasks.[4]   It should be clear, however, from a reading of these early texts that Marx is engaged in giving the concept of alienation a more empirical reference, by depicting a real situation of the worker in industrial society.[5]

---

in the writings of the East German philosopher Wolfgang Harich and of the Polish philosopher Leszek Kolakowski. *See* the latter's essays published in German under the title *Der Mensch ohne Alternative*, Munich, 1960.

[1] In *The Holy Family* Marx observes: " When one studies the materialist theories of the original goodness of man, the equality of intellectual endowment among men, the omnipotence of education, experience and habit, the influence of external circumstances upon man, the great importance of industry, the value of pleasure, etc. it requires no extraordinary insight to discover what necessarily connects them with communism and socialism."

[2] " Economic and Philosophical Manuscripts," pp. 127–9 below.

[3] Ibid., p. 202 below.

[4] Ibid., pp. 124–5 below.

[5] The close connexion between the ideas of Hegel and Marx concerning the self-creation of man through his own activity (cultural as well as material pro-

The empirical value of his observations upon productive work as an element in the mental health and happiness of the individual should be more apparent to us than it was to his contemporaries, although modern sociologists and psychologists have given surprisingly little attention to the subject.[1] In his later writings Marx describes the same situation of the industrial worker, and takes his stand upon the same moral doctrine, without using the term " alienation," which he had doubtless come to regard as unnecessarily metaphysical. It may also be that his confidence in the possibility of making industrial work inherently interesting and satisfying had diminished. In the third volume of *Capital* he writes: " The realm of freedom only begins, in fact, where that labour which is determined by need and external purposes, ceases; . . . [economic production] always remains a realm of necessity. Beyond it begins that development of human potentiality for its own sake, the true realm of freedom . . . " But he also suggests, in the same passage, that within the realm of production itself a certain degree of freedom might be established which would consist in the fact that " socialized

---

duction) and his self-estrangement through the reification of the products of his activity, only became fully apparent with the publication of Hegel's own early manuscripts, especially the *Jenenser Realphilosophie* I, Leipzig, 1932 and II, Leipzig, 1931, and of Marx's " Economic and Philosophical Manuscripts," Berlin, 1932. (For a brief account of Hegel's ideas in the *Realphilosophie, see* H. MARCUSE, *Reason and Revolution*, Part I, Chapter III.) But these manuscripts also help us to see the profound divergence between the two thinkers. Hegel begins, in his early writings, with the accounts of labour in modern capitalist society provided by the early economists and sociological historians (especially Adam Smith and Adam Ferguson) and then proceeds to develop, in his later philosophical system, the notion of labour as the abstract activity of a world spirit. Marx, on the contrary, begins with Hegel's mature philosophy and returns to the empirical accounts of industrial labour given by the economists. It should be added that Marx, as I have noted, incorporated in his conception of man ethical ideas derived from the eighteenth-century French materialists, and from other sources, which were quite foreign to Hegel's thought.

[1] There is an excellent brief discussion in I. MEYERSON, " Le travail, fonction psychologique," *Le travail, les métiers, l'emploi*, Paris, 1955. Georges Friedmann has examined the problem on several occasions, more particularly in the last two chapters of *The Anatomy of Work*, London, 1961; and Erich Fromm has also discussed it in the final chapter of *The Sane Society*, London, 1956.

mankind, the associated producers, regulate their interchange with nature rationally, bring it under their common control instead of being ruled by it as by some blind power, and accomplish their task with the least expenditure of energy and under such conditions as are proper and worthy for human beings "; and at another point, in the first volume of *Capital*, he observes that " the detail worker of today, the limited individual, the mere bearer of a particular social function, will be replaced by the fully developed individual, for whom the different social functions he performs are but so many alternative modes of activity." Whether he emphasizes more strongly the sphere of work, or that of leisure, Marx presents the same ideal conception of man as the fully developed individual who expresses his nature freely in his activity.

Marx's reflections upon alienation began, it is clear, in a more philosophical context. This is most evident in his discussion of religion as a form of alienation, in his use of the term " species-being " which he took from Feuerbach,[1] and in his formulation of the speculative question—which he does not answer—" How does it happen, we may ask, that *man alienates his labour*? How is this alienation founded in the nature of human development? "[2] The study of these early texts has also led, therefore, to a reconsideration of Marx's relation to Hegel. Marcuse[3] and Lukács[4] are among those who regard Marx as having always remained, in some sense, a Hegelian. They insist upon the historical character of Marx's thought, while denying that it constitutes a systematic philosophy of history. For both, it is a system of thought which arises out of, and is mainly concerned with, the social conditions of modern capitalism. Lukács says that " historical materialism, in its classical form, . . . is the *self-consciousness*

---

[1] *See* below, p. 13, note 2.

[2] " Economic and Philosophical Manuscripts," p. 133 below.

[3] H. MARCUSE, *Reason and Revolution*, New York, 1941.

[4] G. LUKÁCS, *Geschichte und Klassenbewusstsein*, Berlin, 1923. In this book Lukács anticipated in some respects a view of Marx's relation to Hegel which could later find support from the " Economic and Philosophical Manuscripts."

of capitalist society. . . . [It is] primarily a theory of bourgeois society and its economic structure." [1] Similarly, Marcuse conceives Marx's thought as a critical theory of capitalism, intimately connected with the situation and activity of the proletariat; " the correct theory is the consciousness of a practice which aims at changing the world." [2] Marx's theory has, therefore, the relativistic character of all historical thought, as Lukács is disposed to admit,[3] and as Marcuse attempts only in a cursory fashion to deny.[4] Marcuse emphasizes the historical and philosophical character of the theory, in contrast with positivistic sociology: " Social study was to be a science seeking social laws, the validity of which was to be analogous to that of physical laws. Social practice, especially the matter of changing the social system, was herewith throttled by the inexorable. Society was viewed as governed by rational laws that moved with a natural necessity. This position directly contradicted the view held by the dialectical social theory, that society is irrational precisely in that it is governed by natural laws. . . . The positivist repudiation of metaphysics was thus coupled with a repudiation of man's claim to alter and reorganize his social institutions in accordance with his rational will." [5]

A similar view—stressing the origins of Marx's thought in the social problems of capitalism—was advanced much earlier by Croce, who concluded that " historical materialism is not and cannot be a new philosophy of history or a new method; but it is properly this; a *mass of new data, of new experiences,* of which the historian becomes conscious. . . . The materialistic view of history arose out of the need to account for a definite social phenomenon [the French Revolution], not from an abstract inquiry into the factors of historical life."[6]

---

[1] Quoted from the French translation, *Histoire et conscience de classe,* Paris, 1960, pp. 263-4.

[2] MARCUSE, op. cit., p. 321. [3] LUKÁCS, op. cit., p. 263.

[4] MARCUSE, op. cit., pp. 321-2. [5] Ibid., pp. 343-4.

[6] BENEDETTO CROCE, *Historical Materialism and the Economics of Karl Marx,* London, 1913, p. 12 and pp. 16-17. The essay from which this quotation is taken was first published in 1896.

A more recent tendency in the discussion of Marx's early thought in relation to Hegel has been to emphasize the religious affinities of the concept of alienation. The attempt has been made, indeed, to portray Marx as essentially a religious thinker.[1] The argument is stated in the following way. Marx held strong moral views, but he was not a moral philosopher; his criticism of capitalist society and his moral vision of the future socialist society both resemble those of a religious thinker. Moreover, this religious conception of the world can be traced back, through Feuerbach, to Hegel—to the idea of man's self-realization as a divine being. This account of Marx's thought achieves two things: it depicts Marx once again as a thoroughgoing Hegelian, and by its emphasis upon one particular aspect of Hegel's thought it also portrays Marx as the creator of a religious myth in a secular form. It succeeds thereby in diminishing his stature as scientist, historian and political thinker.

Does this extreme view of the nature of Marx's thought find any support in his early writings? It is true that Marx reveals himself as a man of intense moral convictions, and as a fervent supporter of the socialist movement at a time when he had not worked out in detail his social theory. It is also true that he does not set forth a coherent moral philosophy. But these facts alone do not make him a religious thinker, nor dispose of the claim that he was above all a scientist. Marx expresses in a different language the moral principles of the Enlightenment, principles which he derived most immediately from Saint-Simon and Feuerbach, but which he later found confirmed by his reading of the economists, and especially of those, such as Schulz and Sismondi, who were early critics of capitalism. The formulations of his moral ideal have no undertones of religious feeling. Marx did not believe that men were, or would become, gods. In the " Economic and Philosophical Manuscripts," and still more in his later writings, he lays stress upon the *human* qualities and failings of

---

[1] R. C. Tucker, *Philosophy and Myth in Karl Marx*, London, 1961.

men. On one occasion, at least, he declared expressly that the socialists do not regard the proletarians as gods, but simply as men who live under inhuman conditions and who are obliged to revolt against this inhumanity.[1] It is a reasonable conjecture that one ground for Marx's dissatisfaction with Feuerbach's philosophy was the excessive part which religious imagery and sentiment still played in it; and that his later distaste for Comte's positive philosophy was due in part to its culmination in a " religion of humanity," to its being, as he noted, " profoundly rooted in Catholic soil."

The cast of Marx's mind was fundamentally scientific. His whole life and work reveal not only a moral passion, but more strikingly a passion for empirical inquiry and factual knowledge. It is this scientific bent, and conversely his distaste for speculative philosophy,[2] which marks most clearly his divergence from Hegel's followers in Germany. In his early writings we see Marx proceeding from a critical examination of Hegelian philosophy to a direct study of the economic and political problems of modern society as they are represented in the works of the economists. He follows the course which he indicates in the " Critique of Hegel's Philosophy of Right "; " . . . the criticism of heaven is transformed into the criticism of earth, the criticism of religion into the criticism of law, and the criticism of theology into the criticism of politics." In the earliest of the texts translated here, " On the Jewish Question," Marx observes, in criticizing Bauer's presentation of the problem: " We do not turn secular questions into theological questions; we turn theological questions into secular ones. . . . The question of the relation between political emancipation and religion becomes for us a question of the relation between political emancipa-

---

[1] In The Holy Family, 1845.

[2] EDMUND WILSON, To the Finland Station (p. 192) quotes Marx's observation that " philosophy stands in the same relation to the study of the actual world as onanism to sexual love." Later in life Marx said to Paul Lafargue " I am not a Marxist "; a remark which I interpret as a protest against the tendency of the early Marxists (amplified by their successors) to transform his concepts and discoveries into a dogmatic philosophical system.

tion and human emancipation. We criticize the religious failings of the political state by criticizing the political state in its secular form, disregarding its religious failings." In the " Critique of Hegel's Philosophy of Right " Marx states more precisely, and in less philosophical language, the object which is to engage his attention: " the relation of industry, of the world of wealth in general, to the political world is a major problem of modern times." The " Economic and Philosophical Manuscripts," finally, show Marx grappling with contemporary economic problems. The completeness of his conversion to this field of study is shown not merely by his long analyses, in the Manuscripts, of wages, profit and rent, and of the conditions of the industrial workers, but also by his notebooks for the whole period 1844–53, which are filled with excerpts from, and commentaries upon, the works of the principal writers upon economic subjects in England, France and Germany.[1]

The reorientation of Marx's thought, after 1843, becomes much clearer if his early writings are seen, as they should be, as a stage in the development of his ideas, rather than as the expression of a distinctive doctrine which has to be brought in to correct our judgement of his later theories. In his early works Marx necessarily employs a philosophical form of expression, since he is engaged in criticizing a mode of thought which is itself philosophical; yet even here the most obvious feature is the transition from philosophical disputation about the nature of man, or of human social development as a whole, to the empirical study of modern economic and political problems. These works look forward to sociological studies of modern capitalism, not backwards to philosophical reflections upon human history. In *Capital*, Marx attempts to explain the origins and course of modern capitalism with the aid of what he considered a scientific theory of social evolution that is akin to the Darwinian theory of biological

---

[1] *See* Maximilien Rubel, " Les cahiers de lecture de Karl Marx, 1840–1853," *International Review of Social History*, I (3) 1957. This article also contains some pertinent observations upon Marx's methods of scientific work.

evolution.[1] At the present day, when we are doubtful about the scientific standing of any theory of evolution as a whole, and especially about the value of the concept of social evolution, we may find much to criticize in Marx's general concepts. But it has still to be said in Marx's favour that he made use of these concepts, in the manner of a scientist, in a profound investigation of one type of society and of one process of social change. Unlike Spencer, and some other early sociologists, he did not propound far-fetched biological analogies, nor attempt to depict the whole evolution of human society on the basis of superficial historical data.

The presentation of Marx's thought by Marcuse and Lukács raises a number of interesting problems which I can only mention very briefly here.[2] Their views are based upon two ideas. The first is that the natural world and the social world are radically different objects, in such a sense that the study of society calls for methods and concepts which are quite different from those employed in the natural sciences. The second is that the attempt to study society by the methods of natural science has, in addition, undesirable practical consequences; for the description of society as it is, and the subsumption of social phenomena under universal laws, encourage a conception of the social world as inalterable by human will. As to the first of these ideas, it should be said that it has been the source of a great variety of criticisms of sociology as a " natural science of society," among which the most substantial is still that which was expounded by Dilthey in his *Einleitung in die Geisteswissenschaften* (1883). Marxism, in the form Marcuse and Lukács preferred, is not, therefore, the most obvious alternative to a positivistic sociology.

---

[1] In the first volume of *Capital*, which he had wished to dedicate to Darwin, Marx himself states the resemblance: " Darwin has aroused our interest in the history of natural technology, i.e. in the formation of the organs of plants and animals, as instruments of production for sustaining life. Does not the history of the productive organs of man, of organs that are the material basis of all social organization, deserve equal attention? "

[2] I shall discuss them in greater detail in a forthcoming volume of essays on Marxism and sociology.

Moreover, as Lukács expounds Marx's method, it is difficult to see how it differs at all from that of Hegel, for the essential features which Lukács mentions [1]—the concepts of " historical process " and of " totality "—are due entirely to Hegel. As to the idea of the inalterability of the social world as depicted by a positive science, this could only be true (i) if sociology claimed to explain the whole social world, and (ii) if, in a psychological sense, the formulation of a social law did actually persuade men to continue acting as the law states that they do (or did) act.

At all events, there is little evidence in Marx's own writings (including the early writings) that he wished to make a radical distinction between the sciences of nature and of man, or that he regarded a positive science of man and society as being incompatible with the practical activity of changing society. On the contrary, like other nineteenth-century thinkers, but in an original manner, he saw a close connexion between humanism (socialism) and positivism (a science of society). As Arnold Toynbee later wrote: " It was the labour question . . . that revived the method of observation. Political Economy was transformed by the working classes." [2] The recent interest in Marx's moral doctrine arises, in great measure, from the deceptions of Marxist socialism. This is, however, a partial view if it neglects to observe that orthodox Marxism has equally abandoned Marx's science of society; and that the latter is Marx's essential contribution both to understanding society and to changing it.

*   *   *

Marx's essay " On the Jewish Question " was written during the autumn of 1843 and was published in the *Deutsch-Französische Jahrbücher* [3] early in 1844.[4]

---

[1] LUKÁCS, op. cit., pp. 17–45 " Qu'est-ce que le marxisme orthodoxe? "
[2] *The Industrial Revolution of the Eighteenth Century in England* (1908 ed.) p. 147.
[3] *Deutsch-Französische Jahrbücher*, edited by K. Marx and A. Ruge, Paris, 1844. Only one double issue of the journal was published, in February 1844.
[4] On pp. 182–214.

The essay entitled " Contribution to the Critique of Hegel's Philosophy of Right. Introduction " was written between the autumn of 1843 and January 1844, and was also published in the *Deutsch-Französische Jahrbücher*.[1]

The title " Economic and Philosophical Manuscripts " has been given to four manuscripts which Marx wrote in the period from April to August 1844, and which are now in the keeping of the International Institute of Social History, Amsterdam. The manuscripts were first published in a full and accurate version, prepared by D. Riazanov, by the Marx-Engels Institute (now the Institute of Marxism-Leninism), Moscow, in *Karl Marx, Friedrich Engels: Historisch-kritische Gesamtausgabe*, Marx-Engels Verlag, Berlin, 1932; Abteilung I, Band III. This edition will be referred to hereafter as the *MEGA*. Each manuscript was separately paginated in Roman numerals by Marx.

The first manuscript comprises nine double sheets (thirty-six pages). Each page is divided by two vertical lines to form three columns, which are headed respectively, " Wages of Labour," " Profit of Capital," and " Rent of Land." These constitute the first three sections of the published text. On page XII of the manuscript, however, Marx began to write on a different subject, ignoring the division of the pages into three columns; this portion of the manuscript was given the title " Alienated Labour " by the editors of the *MEGA*. The manuscript breaks off on page XXVII.

The second manuscript comprises one double sheet (four pages). The text begins in the middle of a sentence, and this is evidently the concluding portion of a manuscript, the rest of which has been lost.

The third manuscript comprises seventeen double sheets (sixty-eight pages). Marx's pagination is faulty; page XXI is followed by page XXIII, and page XXIV is followed by page XXVI. The last twenty-three pages are blank. The manuscript begins with two short sections which refer to

---

[1] On pp. 71–85.

a lost manuscript, and which the editors of the *MEGA* entitled " Private Property and Labour " and " Private Property and Communism " respectively. There follows a section which was given the title " Needs, Production and Division of Labour "; a critique of Hegel's philosophy, which the editors of the *MEGA* placed at the end of the published version in accordance with the indications given in the " Preface "; and the " Preface " itself (beginning on page XXXIX) which was clearly intended to introduce the whole work. On pages XLI–XLIII there is another independent section to which the editors of the *MEGA* gave the title " Money."

The fourth manuscript, comprising one double sheet (four pages), was found sewn into the third manuscript. It contains a résumé of the final chapter, on absolute knowledge, of Hegel's *Phenomenology of Spirit*, and it was published by the editors of the *MEGA* as an appendix to Abteilung I, Band III. Much of the text is used in the criticism of Hegel's philosophy in the third manuscript.

I have used the original publication for my translations of the two essays which Marx himself published in the *Deutsch-Französische Jahrbücher*. For the " Economic and Philosophical Manuscripts " I have used the *MEGA* edition, but have revised the text in a few places. I have not included here the fourth manuscript, since it adds nothing to the discussion of Hegel's philosophy in the third manuscript. I have shown Marx's pagination of the manuscripts by Roman numerals enclosed in square brackets.

Marx quotes extensively, particularly in the " Economic and Philosophical Manuscripts," from the works of English, French and German writers, but he sometimes omits or paraphrases a part of the text. I have restored the original texts of English quotations and have translated French and German quotations from the original texts. I have usually indicated the omissions and paraphrases, but where Marx merely summarizes a passage from another writer I have translated his own text and have referred in a footnote to the original source.

These early writings contain a number of philosophical terms derived from Hegel and Feuerbach; and those parts devoted to criticism of Hegel's philosophy employ many terms to which Hegel (and Marx) gave a technical meaning. In making my translation I have consulted the principal English translations of Hegel's writings, and I have been greatly helped by a recent study of Hegel by J. N. Findlay: *Hegel: A Re-Examination* (London, 1958). It is only necessary to mention here a few of the more common terms. I have translated *Wesen* as " being," " essence," or " life " according to the context; and *aufheben* as " annul " or " abolish " (negative sense) and " supersede " or " transcend " (positive sense). On the other hand I have translated both *Entäusserung* and *Entfremdung* as " alienation " (or occasionally " estrangement ") since Marx (unlike Hegel) does not make a systematic distinction between them; Marx distinguishes between *Entäusserung*, *Entfremdung* (alienation) and *Vergegenständlichung* (objectification).

I have indicated Marx's frequent emphases of certain words and phrases by the use of italics.

My notes to the translations are shown by the sign *Editor's note*, but I have inserted references to the source of quotations without distinguishing them in this way. My notes draw, in some cases, upon the references and critical notes appended to the *MEGA* edition.[1]

---

[1] Including the notes referring to the essays " On the Jewish Question " and " Contribution to the Critique of Hegel's Philosophy of Right. Introduction," both of which are reprinted in the *MEGA* edition, Abteilung I, Band I/1.

ON THE JEWISH QUESTION

1. Bruno Bauer, *Die Judenfrage* (The Jewish Question).

2. Bruno Bauer, " Die Fähigkeit der heutigen Juden und Christen, frei zu werden." (The Capacity of the present-day Jews and Christians to become free.)

1

BRUNO BAUER, *DIE JUDENFRAGE*[1]

THE German Jews seek emancipation. What kind of emancipation do they want? *Civic, political* emancipation.

Bruno Bauer replies to them: In Germany no one is politically emancipated. We ourselves are not free. How then could we liberate you? You Jews are *egoists* if you demand for yourselves, as Jews, a special emancipation. You should work, as Germans, for the political emancipation of Germany, and as men, for the emancipation of mankind. You should feel the particular kind of oppression and shame which you suffer, not as an exception to the rule but rather as a confirmation of the rule.

Or do the Jews want to be placed on a footing of equality with the *Christian subjects*? If they recognize the *Christian state* as legally established they also recognize the régime of general enslavement. Why should their particular yoke be irksome when they accept the general yoke? Why should the German be interested in the liberation of the Jew, if the Jew is not interested in the liberation of the German?

The *Christian* state recognizes nothing but *privileges*. The Jew himself, in this state, has the privilege of being a Jew. As a Jew he possesses rights which the Christians do not have. Why does he want rights which he does not have but which the Christians enjoy?

In demanding his emancipation from the Christian state he asks the Christian state to abandon its *religious* prejudice. But does he, the Jew, give up *his* religious prejudice? Has he then the right to insist that someone else should forswear his religion?

---

[1] Braunschweig, 1843.

The *Christian* state, *by its very nature*, is incapable of emancipating the Jew. But, adds Bauer, the Jew, by his very nature, cannot be emancipated. As long as the state remains Christian, and as long as the Jew remains a Jew, they are equally incapable, the one of conferring emancipation, the other of receiving it.

With respect to the Jews the Christian state can only adopt the attitude of a Christian state. That is, it can permit the Jew, as a matter of privilege, to isolate himself from its other subjects; but it must then allow the pressures of all the other spheres of society to bear upon the Jew, and all the more heavily since he is in *religious* opposition to the dominant religion. But the Jew likewise can only adopt a Jewish attitude, i.e. that of a foreigner, towards the state, since he opposes his illusory nationality to actual nationality, his illusory law to actual law. He considers it his right to separate himself from the rest of humanity; as a matter of principle he takes no part in the historical movement and looks to a future which has nothing in common with the future of mankind as a whole. He regards himself as a member of the Jewish people, and the Jewish people as the chosen people.

On what grounds, then, do you Jews demand emancipation? On account of your religion? But it is the mortal enemy of the state religion. As citizens? But there are no citizens in Germany. As men? But you are not men any more than are those to whom you appeal.

Bauer, after criticizing earlier approaches and solutions, formulates the question of Jewish emancipation in a new way. What, he asks, is the nature of the Jew who is to be emancipated, and the *nature* of the Christian state which is to emancipate him? He replies by a critique of the Jewish religion, analyses the religious opposition between Judaism and Christianity, explains the essence of the Christian state; and does all this with dash, clarity, wit and profundity, in a style which is as precise as it is pithy and vigorous.

How then does Bauer resolve the Jewish question? What is the result? To formulate a question is to resolve it. The critical study of the Jewish question is the answer to the Jewish question. Here it is in brief: we have to emancipate ourselves before we can emancipate others.

The most stubborn form of the opposition between Jew and Christian is the *religious* opposition. How is an opposition resolved? By making it impossible. And how is *religious* opposition made impossible? By abolishing *religion*. As soon as Jew and Christian come to see in their respective religions nothing more than *stages in the development of the human mind*—snake skins which have been cast off by *history*, and *man* as the snake who clothed himself in them— they will no longer find themselves in religious opposition, but in a purely critical, *scientific* and human relationship. *Science* will then constitute their unity. But scientific oppositions are resolved by science itself.

The *German* Jew, in particular, suffers from the general lack of political freedom and the pronounced Christianity of the state. But in Bauer's sense the Jewish question has a general significance, independent of the specifically German conditions. It is the question of the relations between religion and the state, of the *contradiction between religious prejudice and political emancipation*. Emancipation from religion is posited as a condition, both for the Jew who wants political emancipation, and for the state which should emancipate him and itself be emancipated.

" Very well, it may be said (and the Jew himself says it) but the Jew should not be emancipated because he is a Jew, because he has such an excellent and universal moral creed; the *Jew* should take second place to the citizen, and he will be a *citizen* although he is and desires to remain a Jew. In other words, he is and remains a *Jew*, even though he is a *citizen* and as such lives in a universal human condition; his restricted Jewish nature always finally triumphs over his human and political obligations. The bias persists even

though it is overcome by general principles. But if it persists, it would be truer to say that it overcomes all the rest."
" It is only in a sophistical and superficial sense that the Jew could remain a Jew in political life. Consequently, if he wanted to remain a Jew, this would mean that the superficial became the essential and thus triumphed. In other words, his life *in the state* would be only a semblance, or a momentary exception to the essential and normal." [1]

Let us see also how Bauer establishes the role of the state.

" France," he says, " has provided us recently,[2] in connexion with the Jewish question (and for that matter all other *political* questions), with the spectacle of a life which is free but which revokes its freedom by law and so declares it to be merely an appearance; and which, on the other hand, denies its free laws by its acts." [3]

" In France, universal liberty is not yet established by law, nor is the *Jewish question as yet resolved*, because legal liberty, i.e. the equality of all citizens, is restricted in actual life, which is still dominated and fragmented by religious privileges, and because the lack of liberty in actual life influences law in its turn and obliges it to sanction the division of citizens who are by nature free into oppressors and oppressed." [4]

When, therefore, would the Jewish question be resolved in France?

" The Jew would really have ceased to be Jewish, for example, if he did not allow his religious code to prevent his fulfilment of his duties towards the state and his fellow citizens; if he attended and took part in the public business of the Chamber of Deputies on the sabbath. It would be necessary, further, to abolish all *religious privilege*, including the monopoly of a privileged church. If, thereafter, some

---

[1] Bauer, " Die Fähigkeit der heutigen Juden und Christen, frei zu werden," *Einundzwanzig Bogen*, p. 57.   Emphases added by Marx.   [*Editor's note.*]
[2] Chamber of Deputies.   Debate of 26th December, 1840.
[3] Bauer, *Die Judenfrage*, p. 64.
[4] Ibid., p. 65.

or many or *even the overwhelming majority felt obliged to fulfil their religious duties*, such practices should be left *to them as an absolutely* private matter." [1] " There is no longer any religion when there is no longer a privileged religion. Take away from religion its power to excommunicate and it will no longer exist." [2] " Mr. Martin du Nord has seen, in the suggestion to omit any mention of Sunday in the law, a proposal to declare that Christianity has ceased to exist. With equal right (and the right is well founded) the declaration that the law of the sabbath is no longer binding upon the Jew would amount to proclaiming the end of Judaism." [3]

Thus Bauer demands, on the one hand, that the Jew should renounce Judaism, and in general that man should renounce religion, in order to be emancipated as a citizen. On the other hand, he considers, and this follows logically, that the political abolition of religion is the abolition of all religion. The state which presupposes religion is not yet a true or actual state. " Clearly, the religious idea gives some assurances to the state. But to what state? *To what kind of state?*" [4]

At this point we see that the Jewish question is considered only from one aspect.

It was by no means sufficient to ask: who should emancipate? who should be emancipated? The critic should ask a third question: *what kind of emancipation* is involved? What are the essential conditions of the emancipation which is demanded? The criticism of *political emancipation* itself was only the final criticism of the Jewish question and its genuine resolution into the " *general question of the age.*"

Bauer, since he does not formulate the problem at this level, falls into contradictions. He establishes conditions which are not based upon the nature of *political* emancipation. He raises questions which are irrelevant to his

[1] Loc. cit.   [2] BAUER, *Die Judenfrage*, p. 66.
[3] Ibid., p. 71.   [4] Ibid., p. 97.

problem, and he resolves problems which leave his question unanswered. When Bauer says of the opponents of Jewish emancipation that " Their error was simply to assume that the Christian state was the only true one, and not to subject it to the same criticism as Judaism," [1] we see his own error in the fact that he subjects *only* the " Christian state," and not the " state as such " to criticism, that he does not examine *the relation between political emancipation and human emancipation,* and that he, therefore, poses conditions which are only explicable by his lack of critical sense in confusing political emancipation and universal human emancipation. Bauer asks the Jews: Have you, from your standpoint, the right to demand *political emancipation*? We ask the converse question: from the standpoint of *political* emancipation can the Jew be required to abolish Judaism, or man be asked to abolish religion?

The Jewish question presents itself differently according to the state in which the Jew resides. In Germany, where there is no political state, no state as such, the Jewish question is purely *theological*. The Jew finds himself in *religious* opposition to the state, which proclaims Christianity as its foundation. This state is a theologian *ex professo*. Criticism here is criticism of theology; a double-edged criticism, of Christian and of Jewish theology. And so we move always in the domain of theology, however *critically* we may move therein.

In France, which is a *constitutional* state, the Jewish question is a question of constitutionalism, of the incompleteness *of political emancipation*. Since the *semblance* of a state religion is maintained here, if only in the insignificant and self-contradictory formula of a *religion of the majority*, the relation of the Jews to the state also retains a semblance of religious, theological opposition.

It is only in the free states of North America, or at least in some of them, that the Jewish question loses its *theological*

[1] BAUER, *Die Judenfrage*, p. 3.

significance and becomes a truly *secular* question. Only where the state exists in its completely developed form can the relation of the Jew, and of the religious man in general, to the political state appear in a pure form, with its own characteristics. The criticism of this relation ceases to be theological criticism when the state ceases to maintain a *theological* attitude towards religion, that is, when it adopts the attitude of a state, i.e. a *political* attitude. Criticism then becomes *criticism of the political state*. And at this point, where the question ceases to be *theological*, Bauer's criticism ceases to be critical.

" There is not, in the United States, either a state religion or a religion declared to be that of a majority, or a predominance of one religion over another. The state remains aloof from all religions." [1] There are even some states in North America in which " the constitution does not impose any religious belief or practice as a condition of political rights." [2] And yet, " no one in the United States believes that a man without religion can be an honest man." [3] And North America is pre-eminently the country of religiosity, as Beaumont,[4] Tocqueville [5] and the Englishman, Hamilton, [6] assure us in unison. However, the states of North America only serve as an example. The question is: what is the relation between *complete* political emancipation and religion? If we find in the country which has attained full political emancipation, that religion not only continues to *exist* but is *fresh* and *vigorous*, this is proof that the existence of religion is not at all opposed to the perfection of the state. But since the existence of religion is the existence of a defect,

---

[1] GUSTAVE DE BEAUMONT, *Marie ou l'esclavage aux États-Unis*, Bruxelles, 1835, 2 vols., II, p. 207. Marx refers to another edition, Paris, 1835. [*Editor's note*.]

[2] Ibid., p. 216. Beaumont actually refers to *all* the States of North America. [*Editor's note*.]

[3] Ibid., p. 217.   [4] G. DE BEAUMONT, op. cit.

[5] A. DE TOCQUEVILLE, *De la démocratie en Amérique*.

[6] THOMAS HAMILTON, *Men and Manners in North America*, Edinburgh, 1833, 2 vols. Marx quotes from the German translation, Mannheim, 1834. [*Editor's note*.]

the source of this defect must be sought in the *nature* of the
state itself.   Religion no longer appears as the basis, but as
the *manifestation* of secular narrowness.   That is why we
explain the religious constraints upon the free citizens by the
secular constraints upon them.   We do not claim that they
must transcend their religious narrowness in order to get
rid of their secular limitations.   We claim that they will
transcend their religious narrowness once they have overcome their secular limitations.   We do not turn secular
questions into theological questions; we turn theological
questions into secular ones.   History has for long enough
been resolved into superstition; but we now resolve superstition into history.   The question of the *relation between
political emancipation and religion* becomes for us a question of
the *relation between political emancipation and human emancipation.*
We criticize the religious failings of the political state by
criticizing the political state in its *secular* form, disregarding
its religious failings.   We express in human terms the contradiction between the state and a *particular religion,* for
example *Judaism,* by showing the contradiction between the
state and particular *secular elements,* between the state and
religion in general and between the state and its general *presuppositions.*

The *political* emancipation of the Jew or the Christian—of
the *religious* man in general—is the *emancipation of* the state
from Judaism, Christianity, and *religion* in general.   The
state emancipates itself from religion in its own particular
way, in the mode which corresponds to its nature, by
emancipating itself from the *state religion;* that is to say, by
giving recognition to no religion and affirming itself purely
and simply as a state.   To be *politically* emancipated from
religion is not to be finally and completely emancipated from
religion, because political emancipation is not the final and
absolute form of *human* emancipation.

The limits of political emancipation appear at once in the
fact that the *state* can liberate itself from a constraint without

man himself being *really* liberated; that a state may be a *free state* without man himself being a *free man*. Bauer himself tacitly admits this when he makes political emancipation depend upon the following condition—

" It would be necessary, moreover, to abolish all religious privileges, including the monopoly of a privileged church. If some people, or even the *immense majority, still felt obliged to fulfil their religious duties*, this practice should be left to them as a *completely private matter*." Thus the state may have emancipated itself from religion, even though the *immense majority* of people continue to be religious. And the immense majority do not cease to be religious by virtue of being religious *in private*.

The attitude of the state, especially the *free state*, towards religion is only the attitude towards religion of the individuals who compose the state. It follows that man frees himself from a constraint in a *political* way, through the state, when he transcends his limitations, in contradiction with himself, and in an *abstract, narrow* and partial way. Furthermore, by emancipating himself *politically*, man emancipates himself in a *devious way*, through an intermediary, however *necessary* this intermediary may be. Finally, even when he proclaims himself an atheist through the intermediary of the state, that is, when he declares the state to be an atheist, he is still engrossed in religion, because he only recognizes himself as an atheist in a roundabout way, through an intermediary. Religion is simply the recognition of man in a roundabout fashion; that is, through an intermediary. The state is the intermediary between man and human liberty. Just as Christ is the intermediary to whom man attributes all his own divinity and all his religious *bonds*, so the state is the intermediary to which man confides all his non-divinity and all his *human freedom*.

The *political* elevation of man above religion shares the weaknesses and merits of all such political measures. For example, the state as a state abolishes *private property* (i.e. man

decrees by *political* means the *abolition* of private property)
when it abolishes the *property qualification* for electors and
representatives, as has been done in many of the North
American States. Hamilton interprets this phenomenon
quite correctly from the political standpoint: *The masses
have gained a victory over property owners and financial wealth.* [1]
Is not private property ideally abolished when the non-owner
comes to legislate for the owner of property? The *property
qualification* is the last *political* form in which private property
is recognized.

But the political suppression of private property not only
does not abolish private property; it actually presupposes
its existence. The state abolishes, after its fashion, the
distinctions established by *birth, social rank, education, occupation*, when it decrees that birth, social rank, education,
occupation are *non-political* distinctions; when it proclaims,
without regard to these distinctions, that every member of
society is an *equal* partner in popular sovereignty, and treats
all the elements which compose the real life of the nation
from the standpoint of the state. But the state, none the less,
allows private property, education, occupation, to *act* after
their own fashion, namely as private property, education,
occupation, and to manifest their *particular* nature. Far
from abolishing these *effective* differences, it only exists so far
as they are presupposed; it is conscious of being a *political
state* and manifests its *universality* only in opposition to these
elements. Hegel, therefore, defines the relation of the
political state to religion quite correctly when he says: " In
order for the state to come in to existence as the *self-knowing*
ethical actuality of spirit, it is essential that it should be
distinct from the forms of authority and of faith. But this
distinction emerges only in so far as divisions occur within
the ecclesiastical sphere itself. It is only in this way that the
state, above the *particular* churches, has attained to the universality of thought—its formal principle—and is bringing

[1] HAMILTON, op. cit., I, pp. 288, 306, 309.

this universality into existence." [1]   To be sure!   Only in
this manner, *above* the *particular* elements, can the state constitute itself as universality.

The perfected political state is, by its nature, the *species-
life* [2] of man as *opposed* to his material life.   All the presuppositions of this egoistic life continue to exist in *civil
society outside* the political sphere, as qualities of civil society.
Where the political state has attained to its full development,
man leads, not only in thought, in consciousness, but in
reality, in *life*, a double existence—celestial and terrestrial.
He lives in the *political community*, where he regards himself as
a *communal being*, and in *civil society* where he acts simply as a
private individual, treats other men as means, degrades himself
to the role of a mere means, and becomes the plaything of
alien powers.   The political state, in relation to civil society,
is just as spiritual as is heaven in relation to earth.   It stands
in the same opposition to civil society, and overcomes it in
the same manner as religion overcomes the narrowness of
the profane world; i.e. it has always to acknowledge it again,
re-establish it, and allow itself to be dominated by it.   Man,
in his *most intimate* reality, in civil society, is a profane being.
Here, where he appears both to himself and to others as a
real individual he is an *illusory* phenomenon.   In the state,

---

[1] HEGEL, *Grundlinien der Philosophie des Rechts*, Ier Aufgabe, 1821, p. 346.
See the English translation by T. M. KNOX, *Hegel's Philosophy of Right*, Oxford,
1942, p. 173.   [*Editor's note.*]
[2] The terms " species-life " (*Gattungsleben*) and " species-being " (*Gattungs-
wesen*) are derived from Feuerbach.   In the first chapter of *Das Wesen des
Christentums* [*The Essence of Christianity*], Leipzig, 1841, Feuerbach discusses the
nature of man, and argues that man is to be distinguished from animals not by
" consciousness " as such, but by a particular kind of consciousness.   Man is
not only conscious of himself as an individual; he is also conscious of himself
as a member of the human species, and so he apprehends a " human essence "
which is the same in himself and in other men.   According to Feuerbach this
ability to conceive of " species " is the fundamental element in the human
power of reasoning: " Science is the consciousness of species."   Marx, while
not departing from this meaning of the terms, employs them in other contexts;
and he insists more strongly than Feuerbach that since this " species-consciousness " defines the nature of man, man is only living and acting authentically
(i.e. in accordance with his nature) when he lives and acts deliberately as a
" species-being," that is, as a *social* being.   [*Editor's note.*]

on the contrary, where he is regarded as a species-being,[1] man is the imaginary member of an imaginary sovereignty, divested of his real, individual life, and infused with an unreal universality.

The conflict in which the individual, as the professor of a *particular* religion, finds himself involved with his own quality of citizenship and with other men as members of the community, may be resolved into the *secular* schism between the *political* state and *civil society*. For man as a *bourgeois* [2] " life in the state is only an appearance or a fleeting exception to the normal and essential." It is true that the *bourgeois*, like the Jew, participates in political life only in a sophistical way, just as the *citoyen* [3] is a Jew or a *bourgeois* only in a sophistical way. But this sophistry is not personal. It is the *sophistry of the political state* itself. The difference between the religious man and the citizen is the same as that between the shopkeeper and the citizen, between the day-labourer and the citizen, between the landed proprietor and the citizen, between the *living individual* and the *citizen*. The contradiction in which the religious man finds himself with the political man, is the same contradiction in which the *bourgeois* finds himself with the citizen, and the member of civil society with his *political lion's skin*.

This secular opposition, to which the Jewish question reduces itself—the relation between the political state and its presuppositions, whether the latter are material elements such as private property, etc., or spiritual elements such as culture or religion, the conflict between the *general interest* and *private interest*, the schism between the *political* state and *civil society*—these profane contradictions, Bauer leaves intact, while he directs his polemic against their *religious* expression. " It is precisely this basis—that is, the needs which assure the existence of *civil society* and *guarantee its necessity*—which ex-

---

[1] *See* previous note.
[2] I.e. as a member of civil society. [*Editor's note.*]
[3] I.e. the individual with political rights. [*Editor's note.*]

poses its existence to continual danger, maintains an element of uncertainty in civil society, produces this continually changing compound of wealth and poverty, of prosperity and distress, and above all generates change." [1] Compare the whole section entitled " Civil society," [2] which follows closely the distinctive features of Hegel's philosophy of right. Civil society, in its opposition to this political state, is recognized as necessary because the political state is recognized as necessary.

Political emancipation certainly represents a great progress. It is not, indeed, the final form of human emancipation, but it is the final form of human emancipation *within* the framework of the prevailing social order. It goes without saying that we are speaking here of real, practical emancipation.

Man emancipates himself *politically* from religion by expelling it from the sphere of public law to that of private law. Religion is no longer the spirit of the *state*, in which man behaves, albeit in a specific and limited way and in a particular sphere, as a species-being, in community with other men. It has become the spirit of *civil society*, of the sphere of egoism and of the *bellum omnium contra omnes*. It is no longer the essence of *community*, but the essence of *differentiation*. It has become what it was at the *beginning*, an expression of the fact that man is *separated* from the *community*, from himself and from other men. It is now only the abstract avowal of an individual folly, a private whim or caprice. The infinite fragmentation of religion in North America, for example, already gives it the *external* form of a strictly private affair. It has been relegated among the numerous private interests and exiled from the life of the community as such. But one should have no illusions about the scope of political emancipation. The division of man into the *public person* and the *private person*, the *displacement* of religion from the state to civil society—all this is not a

---

[1] BAUER, *Die Judenfrage*, p. 8.   [2] Ibid., pp. 8–9.

stage in political emancipation but its consummation. Thus political emancipation does not abolish, and does not even strive to abolish, man's *real* religiosity.

The *decomposition* of man into Jew and citizen, Protestant and citizen, religious man and citizen, is not a deception practised *against* the political system nor yet an evasion of political emancipation. It is *political emancipation itself*, the *political* mode of emancipation from religion. Certainly, in periods when the political state as such comes violently to birth in civil society, and when men strive to liberate themselves through political emancipation, the state can, and must, proceed to *abolish and destroy religion*; but only in the same way as it proceeds to abolish private property, by declaring a maximum, by confiscation, or by progressive taxation, or in the same way as it proceeds to abolish life, by the *guillotine*. At those times when the state is most aware of itself, political life seeks to stifle its own prerequisites—civil society and its elements—and to establish itself as the genuine and harmonious species-life of man. But it can only achieve this end by setting itself in *violent* contradiction with its own conditions of existence, by declaring a *permanent* revolution. Thus the political drama ends necessarily with the restoration of religion, of private property, of all the elements of civil society, just as war ends with the conclusion of peace.

In fact, the perfected Christian state is not the so-called *Christian* state which acknowledges Christianity as its basis, as the state religion, and thus adopts an exclusive attitude towards other religions; it is, rather, the *atheistic* state, the democratic state, the state which relegates religion among the other elements of civil society. The state which is still theological, which still professes officially the Christian creed, and which has not yet dared to declare itself a *state*, has not yet succeeded in expressing in a *human* and *secular* form, in its political *reality*, the human basis of which Christianity is the transcendental expression. The so-called Christian state is simply a *non-state*; since it is not Christianity as a religion, but only the *human core* of the Christian religion which can realize itself in truly human creations.

The so-called Christian state is the Christian negation of the state, but not at all the political realization of Christianity. The state which professes Christianity as a religion does not yet profess it in a political form, because it still has a religious attitude towards religion. In other words, such a state is not the *genuine realization* of the human basis of religion, because it still accepts the *unreal, imaginary* form of this human core. The so-called Christian state is an *imperfect* state, for which the Christian religion serves as the *supplement* and *sanctification* of its imperfection. Thus religion becomes necessarily one of its *means*; and so it is the *hypocritical* state. There is a great difference between saying: (i) that the *perfect* state, owing to a deficiency in the general *nature* of the state, counts religion as one of its *prerequisites*, or (ii) that the *imperfect* state, owing to a deficiency in its *particular existence* as an imperfect state, declares that religion is its *basis*. In the latter, religion becomes *imperfect politics*. In the former, the imperfection even of perfected *politics* is revealed in religion. The so-called Christian state needs the Christian religion in order to complete itself *as a state*. The democratic state, the real state, does not need religion for its political consummation. On the contrary, it can dispense with religion, because in this case the human core of religion is realized in a profane manner. The so-called Christian state, on the other hand, has a political attitude towards religion, and a religious attitude towards politics. It reduces political institutions and religion equally to mere appearances.

In order to make this contradiction clearer we shall examine Bauer's model of the Christian state, a model which is derived from his study of the German-Christian state.

" Quite recently," says Bauer, " in order to demonstrate the *impossibility* or the *non-existence* of a Christian state, those passages in the Bible have been frequently quoted with which the state *does not conform* and *cannot conform unless it wishes to dissolve itself entirely.*"

" But the question is not so easily settled. What do these Biblical passages demand? Supernatural renunciation, submission to the authority of revelation, turning away from the state, the abolition of profane conditions. But the Christian state proclaims and accomplishes all these things. It has assimilated the *spirit of the Bible,* and if it does not reproduce it exactly in the terms which the Bible uses, that is simply because it expresses this spirit in political forms, in forms which are borrowed from the political system of this world but which, in the religious rebirth which they are obliged to undergo, are reduced to simple appearances. Man turns away from the state and by this means realizes and completes the political institutions." [1]

Bauer continues by showing that the members of a Christian state no longer constitute a nation with a will of its own. The nation has its true existence in the leader to whom it is subjected, but this leader is, by his origin and nature, alien to it since he has been imposed by God without the people having any part in the matter. The laws of such a nation are not its own work, but are direct revelations. The supreme leader, in his relations with the real nation, the masses, requires privileged intermediaries; and the nation itself disintegrates into a multitude of distinct spheres which are formed and determined by chance, are differentiated from each other by their interests and their specific passions and prejudices, and acquire as a privilege the permission to isolate themselves from each other, etc. [2]

But Bauer himself says: " Politics, if it is to be nothing more than religion, should not be politics; any more than the scouring of pans, if it is treated as a religious matter, should be regarded as ordinary housekeeping." [3] But in the German-Christian state religion is an " economic matter " just as " economic matters " are religion. In the German-

---

[1] BAUER, *Die Judenfrage* p. 55.   [2] Ibid., p. 56.   [3] Ibid., p. 108.

Christian state the power of religion is the religion of power.

The separation of the "spirit of the Bible" from the "letter of the Bible" is an *irreligious* act. The state which expresses the Bible in the letter of politics, or in any letter other than that of the Holy Ghost, commits sacrilege, if not in the eyes of men at least in the eyes of its own religion. The state which acknowledges the Bible as its charter and Christianity as its supreme rule must be assessed according to the words of the Bible; for even the language of the Bible is sacred. Such a state, as well as the *human rubbish* upon which it is based, finds itself involved in a painful contradiction, which is insoluble from the standpoint of religious consciousness, when it is referred to those words of the Bible " with which it does not conform and *cannot conform unless it wishes to dissolve itself entirely.*" And why does it not wish to dissolve itself entirely? The state itself cannot answer either itself or others. In its own consciousness the official Christian state is an " ought" whose realization is impossible. It cannot affirm the *reality* of its own existence without lying to itself, and so it remains always in its own eyes an object of doubt, an uncertain and problematic object. Criticism is, therefore, entirely within its rights in forcing the state, which supports itself upon the Bible, into a total disorder of thought in which it no longer knows whether it is *illusion* or *reality*; and in which the infamy of its *profane* ends (for which religion serves as a cloak) enter into an insoluble conflict with the probity of its *religious* consciousness (for which religion appears as the goal of the world). Such a state can only escape its inner torment by becoming the *myrmidon* of the Catholic Church. In the face of this Church, which asserts that secular power is entirely subordinate to its commands, the state is powerless; powerless the secular power which claims to be the rule of the religious spirit.

What prevails in the so-called Christian state is not man but alienation. The only man who counts—the *King*—is

specifically differentiated from other men and is still a religious being associated directly with heaven and with God.
The relations which exist here are relations still based upon
faith. The religious spirit is still not really secularized.

But the religious spirit cannot be *really* secularized. For
what is it but the *non-secular* form of a stage in the development of the human spirit? The religious spirit can only be
realized if the stage of development of the human spirit
which it expresses in religious form, manifests and constitutes
itself in its *secular* form. This is what happens in the *democratic* state. The basis of this state is not Christianity but
the *human basis* of Christianity. Religion remains the ideal,
non-secular consciousness of its members, because it is the
ideal form of the *stage of human development* which has been
attained.

The members of the political state are religious because of
the dualism between individual life and species-life, between
the life of civil society and political life. They are religious
in the sense that man treats political life, which is remote
from his own individual existence, as if it were his true life;
and in the sense that religion is here the spirit of civil society,
and expresses the separation and withdrawal of man from
man. Political democracy is Christian in the sense that man,
not merely one man but every man, is there considered a
sovereign being, a supreme being; but it is uneducated, unsocial man, man just as he is in his fortuitous existence, man
as he has been corrupted, lost to himself, alienated, subjected
to the rule of inhuman conditions and elements, by the whole
organization of our society—in short man who is not yet a
real species-being. Creations of fantasy, dreams, the postulates of Christianity, the sovereignty of man—but of man as
an alien being distinguished from the real man—all these
become, in democracy, the tangible and present reality,
secular maxims.

In the perfected democracy, the religious and theological
consciousness appears to itself all the more religious and

theological in that it is apparently without any political significance or terrestrial aims, is an affair of the heart withdrawn from the world, an expression of the limitations of reason, a product of arbitrariness and fantasy, a veritable life in the beyond. Christianity here attains the *practical* expression of its universal religious significance, because the most varied views are brought together in the form of Christianity, and still more because Christianity does not ask that anyone should profess Christianity, but simply that he should have some kind of religion (*see* Beaumont, op. cit.). The religious consciousness runs riot in a wealth of contradictions and diversity.

We have shown, therefore, that political emancipation from religion leaves religion in existence, although this is no longer a privileged religion. The contradiction in which the adherent of a particular religion finds himself in relation to his citizenship is only *one aspect* of the universal *secular contradiction between the political state and* civil society. The consummation of the Christian state is a state which acknowledges itself simply as a state and ignores the religion of its members. The emancipation of the state from religion is not the emancipation of the real man from religion.

We do not say to the Jews, therefore, as does Bauer: you cannot be emancipated politically without emancipating yourselves completely from Judaism. We say rather: it is because you can be emancipated politically, without renouncing Judaism completely and absolutely, that *political emancipation* itself is not *human* emancipation. If you want to be politically emancipated, without emancipating yourselves humanly, the inadequacy and the contradiction is not entirely in yourselves but in the *nature* and the *category* of political emancipation. If you are preoccupied with this category you share the general prejudice. Just as the state *evangelizes* when, although it is a state, it adopts a Christian attitude towards the Jews, the Jew *acts politically* when, though a Jew, he demands civil rights.

But if a man, though a Jew, can be emancipated politically and acquire civil rights, can he claim and acquire what are called the *rights of man*? Bauer *denies* it. " The question is whether the Jew as such, that is, the Jew who himself avows that he is constrained by his true nature to live eternally separate from men, is able to acquire and to concede to others the *universal rights of man*."

" The idea of the rights of man was only discovered in the Christian world, in the last century. It is not an innate idea; on the contrary, it is acquired in a struggle against the historical traditions in which man has been educated up to the present time. The rights of man are not, therefore, a gift of nature, nor a legacy from past history, but the reward of a struggle against the accident of birth and against the privileges which history has hitherto transmitted from generation to generation. They are the results of culture, and only he can possess them who has merited and earned them."

" But can the Jew really take possession of them? As long as he remains Jewish the limited nature which makes him a Jew must prevail over the human nature which should associate him, as a man, with other men; and it will isolate him from everyone who is not a Jew. He declares, by this separation, that the particular nature which makes him Jewish is his true and supreme nature, before which human nature has to efface itself."

" Similarly, the Christian as such cannot grant the rights of man." [1]

According to Bauer man has to sacrifice the " *privilege of faith* " in order to acquire the general rights of man. Let us consider for a moment the so-called rights of man; let us examine them in their most authentic form, that which they have among those who *discovered* them, the North Americans and the French! These rights of man are, in part, *political* rights, which can only be exercised if one is a member of a

[1] BAUER, *Die Judenfrage*, pp. 19–20.

community. Their content is *participation* in the *community* life, in the *political* life of the community, the life of the state. They fall in the category of *political liberty*, of *civil rights*, which as we have seen do not at all presuppose the consistent and positive abolition of religion; nor consequently, of Judaism. It remains to consider the other part, namely the *rights of man* as distinct from the *rights of the citizen*.

Among them is to be found the freedom of conscience, the right to practise a chosen religion. The *privilege of faith* is expressly recognized, either as a *right of man* or as a consequence of a right of man, namely liberty. *Declaration of the Rights of Man and of the Citizen*, 1791, Article 10: " No one is to be disturbed on account of his opinions, even religious opinions." There is guaranteed, as one of the rights of man, " the liberty of every man to practise the *religion* to which he adheres."

The *Declaration of the Rights of Man, etc.* 1793, enumerates among the rights of man (Article 7): " The liberty of religious observance." Moreover, it is even stated, with respect to the right to express ideas and opinions, to hold meetings, to practise a religion, that: " The necessity of enunciating these *rights* presupposes either the existence or the recent memory of despotism." Compare the Constitution of 1795, Section XII, Article 354.

Constitution of Pennsylvania, Article 9, § 3: " All men have received from nature the imprescriptible *right* to worship the Almighty according to the dictates of their conscience, and no one can be legally compelled to follow, establish or support against his will any religion or religious ministry. No human authority can, in any circumstances, intervene in a matter of conscience or control the forces of the soul."

Constitution of New Hampshire, Articles 5 and 6: " Among these natural rights some are by nature inalienable since nothing can replace them. The rights of conscience are among them." [1]

---

[1] BEAUMONT, op. cit., II, pp. 206–7.

The incompatibility between religion and the rights of man is so little manifest in the concept of the rights of man that the *right to be religious*, in one's own fashion, and to practise one's own particular religion, is expressly included among the rights of man. The privilege of faith is a *universal right of man*.

A distinction is made between the rights of man and the rights of the citizen. Who is this *man* distinct from the *citizen*? No one but the *member of civil society*. Why is the member of civil society called " man," simply man, and why are his rights called the " rights of man "? How is this fact to be explained? By the relation between the political state and civil society, and by the nature of political emancipation.

Let us notice first of all that the so-called *rights of man*, as distinct from the *rights of the citizen*, are simply the rights of a *member of civil society*, that is, of egoistic man, of man separated from other men and from the community. The most radical constitution, that of 1793, says: *Declaration of the Rights of Man and of the Citizen:* Article 2. " These rights, etc. (the natural and imprescriptible rights) are: *equality, liberty, security, property.*

What constitutes liberty?

Article 6. " Liberty is the power which man has to do everything which does not harm the rights of others."

Liberty is, therefore, the right to do everything which does not harm others. The limits within which each individual can act without harming others are determined by law, just as the boundary between two fields is marked by a stake. It is a question of the liberty of man regarded as an isolated monad, withdrawn into himself. Why, according to Bauer, is the Jew not fitted to acquire the rights of man? " As long as he remains Jewish the limited nature which makes him a Jew must prevail over the human nature which should associate him, as a man, with other men; and it will isolate him from everyone who is not a Jew." But liberty as a right of man is not founded upon the relations between man and man, but rather upon the separation of man from man. It is the right of such separation. The right of the *circumscribed* individual, withdrawn into himself.

The practical application of the right of liberty is the right of private property. What constitutes the right of private property?

Article 16 (Constitution of 1793). " The right of *property* is that which belongs to every citizen of enjoying and disposing *as he will* of his goods and revenues, of the fruits of his work and industry."

The right of property is, therefore, the right to enjoy one's fortune and to dispose of it as one will; without regard for other men and independently of society. It is the right of self-interest. This individual liberty, and its application, form the basis of civil society. It leads every man to see in other men, not the *realization*, but rather the *limitation* of his own liberty. It declares above all the right " to enjoy and to dispose of *as one will*, one's goods and revenues, the fruits of one's work and industry."

There remain the other rights of man, equality and security.

The term " equality " has here no political significance. It is only the equal right to liberty as defined above; namely that every man is equally regarded as a self-sufficient monad. The Constitution of 1795 defines the concept of liberty in this sense.

Article 5 (Constitution of 1795). " Equality consists in the fact that the law is the same for all, whether it protects or punishes."

And security?

Article 8 (Constitution of 1793). " Security consists in the protection afforded by society to each of its members for the preservation of his person, his rights, and his property."

Security is the supreme social concept of civil society; the concept of the police. The whole society exists only in order to guarantee for each of its members the preservation of his person, his rights and his property. It is in this sense that Hegel calls civil society " the state of need and of reason."

The concept of security is not enough to raise civil society above its egoism. Security is, rather, the *assurance* of its egoism.

None of the supposed rights of man, therefore, go beyond the egoistic man, man as he is, as a member of civil society; that is, an individual separated from the community, withdrawn into himself, wholly preoccupied with his private interest and acting in accordance with his private caprice. Man is far from being considered, in the rights of man, as a species-being; on the contrary, species-life itself—society—appears as a system which is external to the individual and as a limitation of his original independence. The only bond between men is natural necessity, need and private interest, the preservation of their property and their egoistic persons.

It is difficult enough to understand that a nation which has just begun to liberate itself, to tear down all the barriers between different sections of the people and to establish a political community, should solemnly proclaim (*Declaration* of 1791) the rights of the egoistic man, separated from his fellow men and from the community, and should renew this proclamation at a moment when only the most heroic devotion can save the nation (and is, therefore, urgently called for), and when the sacrifice of all the interests of civil society is in question and egoism should be punished as a crime. (*Declaration of the Rights of Man, etc.* 1793.) The matter becomes still more incomprehensible when we observe that the political liberators reduce citizenship, the *political community*, to a mere *means* for preserving these so-called rights of man; and consequently, that the citizen is declared to be the servant of egoistic " man," that the sphere in which man functions as a species-being is degraded to a level below the sphere where he functions as a partial being, and finally that it is man as a bourgeois and not man as a citizen who is considered the *true* and *authentic* man.

" The end of every *political association* is the *preservation* of the natural and imprescriptible rights of man." (*Declaration of the Rights of Man, etc.* 1791, Article 2.)   " Government is instituted in order to guarantee man's enjoyment of his natural and imprescriptible rights." (*Declaration, etc.* 1793, Article 1.)   Thus, even in the period of its youthful enthusiasm, which is raised to fever pitch by the force of circumstances, political life declares itself to be only a *means*, whose end is the life of civil society.   It is true that its revolutionary practice is in flagrant contradiction with its theory.   While, for instance, security is declared to be one of the rights of man, the violation of the privacy of correspondence is openly considered. While the " unlimited freedom of the Press " (*Constitution* of 1793, Article 122), as a corollary of the right of individual liberty, is guaranteed, the freedom of the Press is completely destroyed, since " the freedom of the Press should not be permitted when it endangers public liberty." [1]   This amounts to saying: the right to liberty ceases to be a right as soon as it comes into conflict with *political* life, whereas in theory political life is no more than the guarantee of the rights of man—the rights of the individual man—and should, therefore, be suspended as soon as it comes into contradiction with its *end*, these rights of man.   But practice is only the exception, while theory is the rule.   Even if one decided to regard revolutionary practice as the correct expression of this relation, the problem would remain as to why it is that in the minds of political liberators the relation is inverted, so that the end appears as the means and the means as the end?   This optical illusion of their consciousness would always remain a problem, though a psychological and theoretical one.

But the problem is easily solved.

Political emancipation is at the same time the *dissolution* of the old society, upon which the sovereign power, the

---

[1] BUCHEZ et ROUX, " Robespierre jeune," *Histoire parlementaire de la Révolution française*, Tome XXVIII, p. 159.

alienated political life of the people, rests. Political revolution is a revolution of civil society. What was the nature of the old society? It can be characterized in one word: *feudalism*. The old civil society had a *directly political* character; that is, the elements of civil life such as property, the family, and types of occupation had been raised, in the form of lordship, caste and guilds, to elements of political life. They determined, in this form, the relation of the individual to the *state as a whole*; that is, his *political* situation, or in other words, his separation and exclusion from the other elements of society. For this organization of national life did not constitute property and labour as social elements; it rather succeeded in *separating* them from the body of the state, and made them *distinct* societies within society. Nevertheless, at least in the feudal sense, the vital functions and conditions of civil society remained political. They excluded the individual from the body of the state, and transformed the *particular* relation which existed between his corporation and the state into a general relation between the individual and social life, just as they transformed his specific civil activity and situation into a general activity and situation. As a result of this organization, the state as a whole and its consciousness, will and activity—the general political power—also necessarily appeared as the *private* affair of a ruler and his servants, separated from the people.

The political revolution which overthrew this power of the ruler, which made state affairs the affairs of the people, and the political state a matter of *general* concern, i.e. a real state, necessarily shattered everything—estates, corporations, guilds, privileges—which expressed the separation of the people from community life. The political revolution therefore *abolished* the *political character of civil society*. It dissolved civil society into its basic elements, on the one hand *individuals*, and on the other hand the *material and cultural elements* which formed the life experience and the civil situation of these individuals. It set free the political spirit which had, so to speak, been dissolved, fragmented and lost in the various culs-de-sac of feudal society; it reassembled these scattered fragments, liberated the political spirit from its connexion with civil life and made of it the community sphere, the *general* concern of the people, in principle independent of these particular elements of civil life. A *specific* activity and situation in life no longer had any but an individual significance. They no longer constituted the general relation between the individual and the state as a whole. Public affairs as such became the general affair of each individual, and political functions became general functions.

But the consummation of the idealism of the state was at the same time the consummation of the materialism of civil society. The bonds which had restrained the egoistic spirit of civil society were removed along with the political yoke. Political emancipation was at the same time an emancipation of civil society from politics and from even the *semblance* of a general content.

Feudal society was dissolved into its basic element, *man*; but into *egoistic* man who was its real foundation.

Man in this aspect, the member of civil society, is now the foundation and presupposition of the *political* state. He is recognized as such in the rights of man.

But the liberty of egoistic man, and the recognition of this liberty, is rather the recognition of the *frenzied* movement of the cultural and material elements which form the content of his life.

Thus man was not liberated from religion; he received religious liberty. He was not liberated from property; he received the liberty to own property. He was not liberated from the egoism of business; he received the liberty to engage in business.

The *formation of the political state*, and the dissolution of civil society into independent *individuals* whose relations are regulated by *law*, as the relations between men in the corporations and guilds were regulated by *privilege*, are accomplished by *one and the same act*. Man as a member of civil society—*non-political* man—necessarily appears as the *natural* man. The rights of man appear as natural rights because *conscious* activity is concentrated upon political *action*. *Egoistic* man is the *passive*, *given* result of the dissolution of society, an object of *direct apprehension* and consequently a *natural* object. The *political revolution* dissolves civil society into its elements without *revolutionizing* these elements themselves or subjecting them to criticism. This revolution regards civil society, the sphere of human needs, labour, private interests and civil law, as the *basis of its own existence*, as a self-subsistent *precondition*, and thus as its *natural basis*. Finally, man as a member of civil society is identified with *authentic man*, *man* as distinct from citizen, because he is man in his sensuous, individual and *immediate* existence, whereas *political* man is only abstract, artificial man, man as an *allegorical*, *moral* person. Thus man as he really is, is seen only in the form of *egoistic* man, and man in his *true* nature only in the form of the *abstract citizen*.

The abstract notion of political man is well formulated by Rousseau: " Whoever dares undertake to establish a people's institutions must feel himself capable of *changing*, as it were, *human nature* itself, of *transforming* each individual who, in isolation, is a complete but solitary whole, into a *part* of something greater than himself, from which in a sense, he derives his life and his being; [of changing man's nature in order to strengthen it;] of substituting a limited and moral existence for the physical and independent life [with which all of us are endowed by nature]. His task, in short, is to take from *a man his own powers*, and to give him in exchange alien powers which he can only employ with the help of other men." [1]

---

[1] J. J. ROUSSEAU, *Du contrat social*, Book II. Chapter VII, " The Legislator." Marx quoted this passage in French, and added the emphases; he omitted the portions enclosed in square brackets. [*Editor's note.*]

Every emancipation is a *restoration* of the human world and of human relationships to *man himself*.

Political emancipation is a reduction of man, on the one hand to a member of civil society, an *independent* and *egoistic* individual, and on the other hand, to a *citizen*, to a moral person.

Human emancipation will only be complete when the real, individual man has absorbed into himself the abstract citizen; when as an individual man, in his everyday life, in his work, and in his relationships, he has become a *species-being*; and when he has recognized and organized his own powers (*forces propres*) as *social* powers so that he no longer separates this social power from himself as *political* power.

BRUNO BAUER, "DIE FÄHIGKEIT DER HEUTIGEN JUDEN UND CHRISTEN, FREI ZU WERDEN."[1]

IT is in this form that Bauer studies the relation between the *Jewish and Christian religions*, and also their relation with modern criticism. This latter relation is their relation with " the capacity to become free."

He reaches this conclusion: " The Christian has only to raise himself one degree, to rise above his religion, in order to abolish religion in general," and thus to become free; but " the Jew, on the contrary, has to break not only with his Jewish nature, but also with the process towards the consummation of his religion, a process which has remained alien to him." [2]

Thus Bauer here transforms the question of Jewish emancipation into a purely religious question. The theological doubt about whether the Jew or the Christian has the better chance of attaining salvation is reproduced here in the more enlightened form: which of the two is more *capable of emancipation*? It is indeed no longer asked: which makes free—Judaism or Christianity? On the contrary, it is now asked: which makes free—the negation of Judaism or the negation of Christianity?

" If they wish to become free the Jews should not embrace Christianity as such, but Christianity in dissolution, religion in dissolution; that is to say, the Enlightment, criticism, and its outcome, a free humanity." [3]

It is still a matter, therefore, of the Jews professing some

---

[1] [The capacity of the present-day Jews and Christians to become free.] In *Einundzwanzig Bogen aus der Schweiz* (Ed. G. Herwegh), pp. 56–71.

[2] Loc. cit., p. 71.

[3] Ibid., p. 70.

kind of faith; no longer Christianity as such, but Christianity in dissolution.

Bauer asks the Jews to break with the essence of the Christian religion, but this demand does not follow, as he himself admits, from the development of the Jewish nature.

From the moment when Bauer, at the end of his *Judenfrage*, saw in Judaism only a crude religious criticism of Christianity, and, therefore, attributed to it only a religious significance, it was to be expected that he would transform the emancipation of the Jews into a philosophico-theological act.

Bauer regards the *ideal* and abstract essence of the Jew— his *religion*—as the *whole* of his nature. He, therefore, concludes rightly that " The Jew contributes nothing to mankind when he disregards his own limited law," when he renounces all his Judaism.[1]

The relation between Jews and Christians thus becomes the following: the only interest which the emancipation of the Jew presents for the Christian is a general human and *theoretical* interest. Judaism is a phenomenon which offends the religious eye of the Christian. As soon as the Christian's eye ceases to be religious the phenomenon ceases to offend it. The emancipation of the Jew is not in itself, therefore, a task which falls to the Christian to perform.

The Jew, on the other hand, if he wants to emancipate himself has to undertake, besides his own work, the work of the Christian—the " criticism of the gospels," of the " life of Jesus," etc.[2]

" It is for them to arrange matters; they will decide their own destiny. But history does not allow itself to be mocked." [3]

---

[1] Loc. cit., p. 65.

Marx alludes here to BRUNO BAUER, *Kritik der evangelischen Geschichte der Synoptiker*, Vols. I–II, Leipzig, 1841; Vol. III, Braunschweig, 1842, and DAVID FRIEDRICH STRAUSS, *Das Leben Jesu*, 2 vols. Tübingen, 1835–6. An English translation of Strauss' book by Marian Evans (George Eliot) was published in 1846 under the title *Life of Jesus Critically Examined*. [*Editor's note*.]

[3] BAUER, " Die Fähigkeit . . . etc.," p. 71.

We will attempt to escape from the theological formulation of the question. For us, the question concerning the
capacity of the Jew for emancipation is transformed into
another question: what specific *social* element is it necessary
to overcome in order to abolish Judaism? For the capacity
of the present-day Jew to emancipate himself expresses the
relation of Judaism to the emancipation of the contemporary
world. The relation results necessarily from the particular
situation of Judaism in the present enslaved world.

Let us consider the real Jew: not the *sabbath Jew*, whom
Bauer considers, but the *everyday Jew*.

Let us not seek the secret of the Jew in his religion, but let
us seek the secret of the religion in the real Jew.

What is the profane basis of Judaism? *Practical* need, *self-
interest*. What is the worldly cult of the Jew? *Huckstering*.
What is his worldly god? *Money*.

Very well: then in emancipating itself from *huckstering* and
money, and thus from real and practical Judaism, our age
would emancipate itself.

An organization of society which would abolish the pre-
conditions and thus the very possibility of huckstering, would
make the Jew impossible. His religious consciousness would
evaporate like some insipid vapour in the real, life-giving air
of society. On the other hand, when the Jew recognizes his
practical nature as invalid and endeavours to abolish it, he
begins to deviate from his former path of development,
works for general *human emancipation* and turns against the
supreme practical expression of human self-estrangement.

We discern in Judaism, therefore, a universal *antisocial*
element of the *present time*, whose historical development,
zealously aided in its harmful aspects by the Jews, has now
attained its culminating point, a point at which it must
necessarily begin to disintegrate.

In the final analysis, the *emancipation of* the Jews is the
emancipation of mankind from *Judaism*.

The Jew has already emancipated himself in a Jewish

fashion. " The Jew, who is merely tolerated in Vienna for example, determines the fate of the whole Empire by his financial power. The Jew, who may be entirely without rights in the smallest German state, decides the destiny of Europe. While the corporations and guilds exclude the Jew, or at least look on him with disfavour, the audacity of industry mocks the obstinacy of medieval institutions." [1]

This is not an isolated instance. The Jew has emancipated himself in a Jewish manner, not only by acquiring the power of money, but also because *money* had become, through him and also apart from him, a world power, while the practical Jewish spirit has become the practical spirit of the Christian nations. The Jews have emancipated themselves in so far as the Christians have become Jews.

Thus, for example, Captain Hamilton reports that the devout and politically free inhabitant of New England is a kind of Laocoon who makes not the least effort to escape from the serpents which are crushing him. *Mammon* is his idol which he adores not only with his lips but with the whole force of his body and mind. In his view the world is no more than a Stock Exchange, and he is convinced that he has no other destiny here below than to become richer than his neighbour. Trade has seized upon all his thoughts, and he has no other recreation than to exchange objects. When he travels he carries, so to speak, his goods and his counter on his back and talks only of interest and profit. If he loses sight of his own business for an instant it is only in order to pry into the business of his competitors. [2]

In North America, indeed, the effective domination of the Christian world by Judaism has come to be manifested in a common and unambiguous form; the *preaching of the Gospel* itself, Christian preaching, has become an article of commerce, and the bankrupt trader in the church behaves like the prosperous clergyman in business. " This man whom

[1] BAUER, *Die Judenfrage*, p. 14.
[2] HAMILTON, op. cit., I, p. 213. Marx paraphrases this passage. [*Editor's note.*]

you see at the head of a respectable congregation began as a
trader; his business having failed he has become a minister.
This other began as a priest, but as soon as he had accumulated some money he abandoned the priesthood for trade.
In the eyes of many people the religious ministry is a veritable
industrial career." [1]

According to Bauer, it is " a hypocritical situation when,
in theory, the Jew is deprived of political rights, while in
practice he wields tremendous power and exercises on a
wholesale scale the political influence which is denied him in
minor matters." [2]

The contradiction which exists between the effective
political power of the Jew and his political rights, is the
contradiction between politics and the power of money in
general.   Politics is in principle superior to the power of
money, but in practice it has become its bondsman.

Judaism has maintained itself *alongside* Christianity, not
only because it constituted the religious criticism of
Christianity and embodied the doubt concerning the religious origins of Christianity, but equally because the
practical Jewish spirit—Judaism or commerce [3]—has per-
petuated itself in Christian society and has even attained its
highest development there.   The Jew, who occupies a
distinctive place in civil society, only manifests in a distinctive
way the Judaism of civil society.

Judaism has been preserved, not in spite of history, but by
history.

It is from its own entrails that civil society ceaselessly
engenders the Jew.

What was, in itself, the basis of the Jewish religion?
Practical need, egoism.

The monotheism of the Jews is, therefore, in reality, a

[1] BEAUMONT, op. cit., II, p. 179.
[2] BAUER, *Die Judenfrage*, p. 14.
[3] The German word *Judentum* had, in the language of the time, the secondary meaning of " commerce," and in this and other passages Marx exploits the
two senses of the word.   [*Editor's note.*]

polytheism of the numerous needs of man, a polytheism which makes even the lavatory an object of divine regulation. *Practical need, egoism,* is the principle of *civil society,* and is revealed as such in its pure form as soon as civil society has fully engendered the political state. The god of *practical need and self-interest* is *money.*

Money is the jealous god of Israel, beside which no other god may exist. Money abases all the gods of mankind and changes them into commodities. Money is the universal and self-sufficient *value* of all things. It has, therefore, deprived the whole world, both the human world and nature, of their own proper value. Money is the alienated essence of man's work and existence; this essence dominates him and he worships it.

The god of the Jews has been secularized and has become the god of this world. The bill of exchange is the real god of the Jew. His god is only an illusory bill of exchange.

The mode of perceiving nature, under the rule of private property and money, is a real contempt for, and a practical degradation of, nature, which does indeed exist in the Jewish religion but only as a creature of the imagination.

It is in this sense that Thomas Münzer declares it intolerable " that every creature should be transformed into property—the fishes in the water, the birds of the air, the plants of the earth: the creature too should become free." [1]

That which is contained in an abstract form in the Jewish religion—contempt for theory, for art, for history, and for man as an end in himself—is the *real, conscious* standpoint and the virtue of the man of money. Even the species-relation itself, the relation between man and woman, becomes an object of commerce. Woman is bartered away.

---

[1] Quoted from Thomas Münzer's pamphlet against Luther, " Hochverrusachte Schutzrede und Antwort wider das geistlose, sanftlebende Fleisch zu Wittenberg, welches mit verkehrter Weise durch den Diebstahl der heiligen Schrift die erbärmliche Christenheit also ganz jämmerlich besudelt hat." (p. B. iii. 1524.)

The *chimerical* nationality of the Jew is the nationality of the trader, and above all of the financier.

The law, without basis or reason, of the Jew, is only the religious caricature of morality and right in general, without basis or reason; the purely *formal* rites with which the world of self-interest encircles itself.

Here again the supreme condition of man is his *legal* status, his relationship to laws which are valid for him, not because they are the laws of his own will and nature, but because they are dominant and any infraction of them will be *avenged*.

Jewish Jesuitism, the same practical Jesuitism which Bauer discovers in the Talmud, is the relationship of the world of self-interest to the laws which govern this world, laws which the world devotes its principal arts to circumventing.

Indeed, the operation of this world within its framework of laws is impossible without the continual supersession of law.

Judaism could not develop further as a *religion*, in a theoretical form, because the world view of practical need is, by its very nature, circumscribed, and the delineation of its characteristics soon completed.

The religion of practical need could not, by its very nature, find its consummation in theory, but only in *practice*, just because practice is its truth.

Judaism could not create a new world. It could only bring the new creations and conditions of the world within its own sphere of activity, because practical need, the spirit of which is self-interest, is always passive, cannot expand at will, but *finds* itself extended as a result of the continued development of society.

Judaism attains its apogee with the perfection of civil society; but civil society only reaches perfection in the *Christian* world. Only under the sway of Christianity, which *objectifies all* national, natural, moral and theoretical relationships, could civil society separate itself completely from the life of the state, sever all the species-bonds of man, establish egoism and selfish need in their place, and dissolve the human world into a world of atomistic, antagonistic individuals.

Christianity issued from Judaism. It has now been re-absorbed into Judaism.

From the beginning, the Christian was the theorizing Jew; consequently, the Jew is the practical Christian. And the practical Christian has become a Jew again.

It was only in appearance that Christianity overcame real Judaism. It was too *refined*, too spiritual to eliminate the crudeness of practical need except by raising it into the ethereal realm.

Christianity is the sublime thought of Judaism; Judaism is the vulgar practical application of Christianity. But this practical application could only become universal when Christianity as perfected religion had accomplished, in a *theoretical* fashion, the alienation of man from himself and from nature.

It was only then that Judaism could attain universal domination and could turn alienated man and alienated nature into *alienable*, saleable objects, in thrall to egoistic need and huckstering.

Objectification is the practice of alienation. Just as man, so long as he is engrossed in religion, can only objectify his essence by an *alien* and fantastic being; so under the sway of egoistic need, he can only affirm himself and produce objects in practice by subordinating his products and his own activity to the domination of an alien entity, and by attributing to them the significance of an alien entity, namely money.

In its perfected practice the spiritual egoism of Christianity necessarily becomes the material egoism of the Jew, celestial need is transmuted into terrestrial need, subjectivism into self-interest. The tenacity of the Jew is to be explained, not by his religion, but rather by the human basis of his religion —practical need and egoism.

It is because the essence of the Jew was universally realized and secularized in civil society, that civil society could not convince the Jew of the *unreality* of his *religious* essence, which is precisely the ideal representation of practical need. It is not only, therefore, in the Pentateuch and the Talmud, but also in contemporary society, that we find the essence of the present-day Jew; not as an abstract essence, but as one which is supremely empirical, not only as a limitation of the Jew, but as the Jewish narrowness of society.

As soon as society succeeds in abolishing the *empirical* essence of Judaism—huckstering and its conditions—the Jew becomes *impossible*, because his consciousness no longer has an object. The subjective basis of Judaism—practical need—assumes a human form, and the conflict between the individual, sensuous existence of man and his species-existence, is abolished.

The *social* emancipation of the Jew is the *emancipation of society from Judaism*.

CONTRIBUTION TO THE CRITIQUE OF HEGEL'S PHILOSOPHY OF RIGHT

INTRODUCTION

CONTRIBUTION TO THE CRITIQUE OF HEGEL'S PHILOSOPHY OF RIGHT

INTRODUCTION

FOR Germany, the *criticism of religion* has been largely completed; and the criticism of religion is the premise of all criticism.

The *profane* existence of error is compromised once its *celestial oratio pro aris et focis* has been refuted. Man, who has found in the fantastic reality of heaven, where he sought a supernatural being, only his own reflection, will no longer be tempted to find only the *semblance* of himself—a non-human being—where he seeks and must seek his true reality.

The basis of irreligious criticism is this: *man makes religion*; religion does not make man. Religion is indeed man's self-consciousness and self-awareness so long as he has not found himself or has lost himself again. But *man* is not an abstract being, squatting outside the world. Man is *the human world*, the state, society. This state, this society, produce religion which is an *inverted world consciousness*, because they are an *inverted world*. Religion is the general theory of this world, its encyclopedic compendium, its logic in popular form, its spiritual *point d'honneur*, its enthusiasm, its moral sanction, its solemn complement, its general basis of consolation and justification. It is *the fantastic realization* of the human being inasmuch as the *human being* possesses no true reality. The struggle against religion is, therefore, indirectly a struggle against *that world* whose spiritual *aroma* is religion.

Religious suffering is at the same time an *expression* of real suffering and a *protest* against real suffering. Religion is the sigh of the oppressed creature, the sentiment of a heartless world, and the soul of soulless conditions.　It is the *opium* of the people.

The abolition of religion as the *illusory* happiness of men, is a demand for their *real* happiness.　The call to abandon their illusions about their condition is a *call to abandon a condition which requires illusions*.　The criticism of religion is, therefore, *the embryonic criticism of this vale of tears* of which religion is the *halo*.

Criticism has plucked the imaginary flowers from the chain, not in order that man shall bear the chain without caprice or consolation but so that he shall cast off the chain and pluck the living flower.　The criticism of religion disillusions man so that he will think, act and fashion his reality as a man who has lost his illusions and regained his reason; so that he will revolve about himself as his own true sun.　Religion is only the illusory sun about which man revolves so long as he does not revolve about himself.

It is the *task of history*, therefore, once the *other-world of truth* has vanished, to establish the *truth of this world*.　The immediate *task of philosophy*, which is in the service of history, is to unmask human self-alienation in its *secular form* now that it has been unmasked in its *sacred form*.　Thus the criticism of heaven is transformed into the criticism of earth, the *criticism of religion* into the *criticism of law*, and the *criticism of theology* into the *criticism of politics*.

The following exposition [1]—which is a contribution to this undertaking—does not deal directly with the original but with a copy, the German *philosophy* of the state and of right, for the simple reason that it deals with Germany.

If one were to begin with the *status quo* itself in Germany, even in the most appropriate way, i.e. negatively, the result

---

[1] Marx refers to his intention to publish a critical study of Hegel's *Philosophy of Right*, to which this essay was an introduction.　One of Marx's preliminary manuscripts for such a study has been published entitled " Aus der Kritik der Hegelschen Rechtsphilosophie.　Kritik des Hegelschen Staatsrechts." (*MEGA* I i i, pp. 403–553.)　The "Economic and Philosophical Manuscripts" is another version of this study; *see* Marx's comment (p. 63 below).　[*Editor's note.*]

would still be an *anachronism*. Even the negation of our political present is already a dusty fact in the historical lumber room of modern nations. I may negate powdered wigs, but I am still left with unpowdered wigs. If I negate the German situation of 1843 I have, according to French chronology, hardly reached the year 1789, and still less the vital centre of the present day.

German history, indeed, prides itself upon a development which no other nation had previously accomplished, or will ever imitate in the historical sphere. We have shared in the restorations of modern nations without ever sharing in their revolutions. We have been restored, first because other nations have dared to make revolutions, and secondly because other nations have suffered counter-revolutions; in the first case because our masters were afraid, and in the second case because they were not afraid. Led by our shepherds, we have only once kept company with liberty and that was on the *day of its internment*.

A school of thought, which justifies the infamy of today by that of yesterday, which regards every cry from the serf under the knout as a cry of rebellion once the knout has become time-honoured, ancestral and historical, a school for which history shows only its *a posteriori* as the God of Israel did for his servant Moses—the *Historical school of law* [1]—might be supposed to have invented German history, if it were not in fact itself an invention of German history. A Shylock, but a servile Shylock, it swears upon its bond, its historical, Christian-Germanic bond, for every pound of flesh cut from the heart of the people.

[1] The principal representative of the Historical school was F. K. von Savigny (1779–1861) who outlined its programme in his book *Vom Beruf unserer Zeit für Gesetzgebung und Rechtswissenschaft* (On the Vocation of our Age for Legislation and Jurisprudence), Heidelberg, 1814. Marx attended Savigny's lectures at the University of Berlin in 1836–7; but he was more attracted by the lectures of Eduard Gans (1798–1839), a liberal Hegelian influenced by Saint-Simon, who emphasized in his teaching and writings the part played by reason in the development of law, and who was Savigny's principal opponent in Berlin. [*Editor's note.*]

On the other hand, good-natured enthusiasts, German chauvinists by temperament and enlightened liberals by reflection, seek our history of liberty beyond our history, in the primeval Teutonic forests. But how does the history of our liberty differ from the history of the wild boar's liberty, if it is only to be found in the forests? And as the proverb has it: what is shouted into the forest, the forest echoes back. So peace upon the primeval Teutonic forests!

But *war* upon the state of affairs in Germany! By all means! This state of affairs is *beneath the level of history, beneath all criticism*; nevertheless it remains an object of criticism just as the criminal who is beneath humanity remains an object of the *executioner*. In its struggle against this state of affairs criticism is not a passion of the head, but the head of passion. It is not a lancet but a weapon. Its object is an *enemy* which it aims not to refute but to *destroy*. For the spirit of this state of affairs has already been refuted. It is not, in itself, an object worthy of our thought; it is an *existence* as contemptible as it is despised. Criticism itself has no need of any further elucidation of this object, for it has already understood it. Criticism is no longer an end in itself, but simply a means; *indignation* is its essential mode of feeling, and *denunciation* its principal task.

It is a matter of depicting the stifling pressure which the different social spheres exert upon each other, the universal but passive ill-humour, the complacent but self-deluding narrowness of spirit; all this incorporated in a system of government which lives by conserving this paltriness, and is itself *paltriness in government*.

What a spectacle! Society is infinitely divided into the most diverse races, which confront each other with their petty antipathies, bad conscience and coarse mediocrity; and which, precisely because of their ambiguous and mistrustful situation, are treated without exception, though in different ways, as merely tolerated existences by their masters. And they are forced to recognize and acknowledge this fact of being *dominated, governed* and *possessed,* as a *concession from heaven!* On the other side are the rulers themselves, whose greatness is in inverse proportion to their number.

The criticism which deals with this subject-matter is criticism in a hand-to-hand fight; and in such a fight it is of no interest to know whether the adversary is of the same rank, is noble or *interesting*—all that matters is to *strike* him. It is a question of denying the Germans an instant of illusion or resignation. The burden must be made still more irksome by awakening a consciousness of it, and shame must be made more shameful still by rendering it public. Every sphere of German society must be depicted as the *partie honteuse* of German society; and these petrified social conditions must be made to dance by singing their own melody to them. The nation must be taught to be *terrified* of itself, in order to give it *courage.* In this way an imperious need of the German nation will be satisfied, and the needs of nations are themselves the final causes of their satisfaction.

Even for the modern nations this struggle against the limited character of the German *status quo* does not lack interest; for the German *status quo* is the open *consummation of the ancien régime,* and the *ancien régime* is the *hidden defect of the modern state.* The struggle against the political present of the Germans is a struggle against the past of the modern nations, who are still continually importuned by the reminiscences of this past. It is instructive for the modern nations to see the *ancien régime,* which has played a *tragic* part in their history, play a *comic* part as a German ghost. The *ancien régime* had a *tragic* history, so long as it was the established power in the world while liberty was a personal fancy; in short, so long as it believed and had to believe in its own validity. So long as the *ancien régime,* as an existing world order, struggled against a new world which was just coming into existence, there was on its side a historical error but no personal error. Its decline was, therefore, tragic.

The present German régime, on the other hand, which is an anachronism, a flagrant contradiction of universally accepted axioms—the nullity of the *ancien régime* revealed to the whole world—only imagines that it believes in itself and asks the world to share its illusion. If it believed in its own *nature* would it attempt to hide it beneath the *semblance* of an alien nature and look for its salvation in hypocrisy and sophistry? The modern *ancien régime* is the comedian of a world order whose *real heroes* are dead. History is thorough, and it goes through many stages when it conducts an ancient formation to its grave. The last stage of a world-historical formation is comedy. The Greek gods, already once mortally wounded in Aeschylus' tragedy *Prometheus Bound*, had to endure a second death, a comic death, in Lucian's dialogues. Why should history proceed in this way? So that mankind shall separate itself *gladly* from its past. We claim this *joyful* historical destiny for the political powers of Germany.

But as soon as criticism concerns itself with modern social and political reality, and thus arrives at genuine human problems, it must either go outside the German *status quo* or approach its object indirectly. For example, the relation of industry, of the world of wealth in general, to the political world is a major problem of modern times. In what form does this problem begin to preoccupy the Germans? In the form of *protective tariffs*, the *system of prohibition*, the *national economy*. German chauvinism has passed from men to matter, so that one fine day our knights of cotton and heroes of iron found themselves metamorphosed into patriots. The sovereignty of monopoly within the country has begun to be recognized since *sovereignty vis-à-vis foreign countries* was attributed to it. In Germany, therefore, a beginning is made with what came as the conclusion in France and England. The old, rotten order against which these nations revolt in their theories, and which they bear only as chains are borne, is hailed in Germany as the dawn of a glorious future which as yet hardly dares to move from a cunning [1] theory to a ruthless practice.   While in France and England the problem is put in the form: *political economy* or the *rule of society over wealth*; in Germany it is put in the form: *national economy* or the *rule of private property over nationality*.   Thus, in England and France it is a question of abolishing monopoly, which has developed to its final consequences; while in Germany it is a question of proceeding to the final consequences of monopoly.   There it is a question of the solution; here, only a question of the collision.   We can see very well from this example how modern problems are presented in Germany; the example shows that our history, like a raw recruit, has so far only had to do extra drill on old and hackneyed historical matters.

If the *whole* of German development were at the level of German *political* development, a German could have no greater part in contemporary problems than can a *Russian*. If the individual is not restricted by the limitations of his country, still less is the nation liberated by the liberation of one individual.   The fact that a Scythian was one of the Greek philosophers [2] did not enable the Scythians to advance a single step towards Greek culture.

Fortunately, we Germans are not Scythians.

Just as the nations of the ancient world lived their pre-history in the imagination, in mythology, so we Germans have lived our post-history in thought, in *philosophy*.   We are the *philosophical* contemporaries of the present day without being its *historical* contemporaries.   German philosophy is the *ideal prolongation* of German history.   When, therefore, we criticize, instead of the *oeuvres incomplètes* of our real history, the *oeuvres posthumes* of our ideal history—*philosophy*, our criticism stands at the centre of the problems of which the

---

[1] In German, *listigen*; Marx is punning upon the name of Friedrich List (1789–1846), the apostle of industrial capitalism in a nationalist and protectionist form, who published in 1840 his influential book, *Das nationale System der politischen Ökonomie*.   [*Editor's note.*]

[2] Anacharsis.   [*Editor's note.*]

present age says: *that is the question.* That which constitutes, for the advanced nations, a *practical* break with modern political conditions, is in Germany where these conditions do not yet exist, virtually a *critical* break with their philosophical reflection.

The German *philosophy of right and of the state* is the only German history which is *al pari* with the *official* modern times. The German nation is obliged, therefore, to connect its dream history with its present conditions, and to subject to criticism not only these existing conditions but also their abstract continuation. Its future cannot be restricted either to the direct negation of its real juridical and political circumstances, or to the direct realization of its ideal juridical and political circumstances. The direct negation of its real circumstances already exists in its ideal circumstances, while it has almost outlived the realization of its ideal circumstances in the contemplation of neighbouring nations. It is with good reason, therefore, that the *practical* political party in Germany demands the *negation of philosophy.* Its error does not consist in formulating this demand, but in limiting itself to a demand which it does not, and cannot, make effective. It supposes that it can achieve this negation by turning its back on philosophy, looking elsewhere, and murmuring a few trite and ill-humoured phrases. Because of its narrow outlook it does not take account of philosophy as part of *German* reality, and even regards philosophy as beneath the level of German practical life and its theories. You demand as a point of departure real germs of life, but you forget that the real germ of life of the German nation has so far sprouted only in its *cranium.* In short, *you cannot abolish philosophy without realizing it.*

The same error was committed, but in the opposite direction, by the *theoretical* party which originated in philosophy.

In the present struggle, this party saw *only* the *critical struggle of philosophy against the German world.* It did not consider that *previous philosophy* itself belongs to this world and is its complement, even if only an ideal complement.   Critical as regards its counterpart, it was not self-critical.   It took as its point of departure the *presuppositions* of philosophy; and either accepted the conclusions which philosophy had reached or else presented as direct philosophical demands and conclusions, demands and conclusions drawn from elsewhere.   But these latter—assuming their legitimacy—can only be achieved by the *negation of previous philosophy*, that is, philosophy as philosophy.   We shall provide later a more comprehensive account of this party.   Its principal defect may be summarized as follows: *it believed that it could realize philosophy without abolishing it.*

The criticism of the *German philosophy of right and of the state* which was given its most logical, profound and complete expression by Hegel, is at once the critical analysis of the modern state and of the reality connected with it, and the definitive negation of all the past *forms of consciousness in German jurisprudence and politics*, whose most distinguished and most general expression, raised to the level of a *science*, is precisely the *speculative philosophy of right*.   If it was only Germany which could produce the speculative philosophy of right—this extravagant and abstract thought about the modern state, the reality of which remains in the beyond (even if this beyond is only across the Rhine)—the *German* representative of the modern state, on the contrary, which leaves out of account the *real man* was itself only possible because, and to the extent that, the modern state itself leaves the *real man* out of account or only satisfies the *whole* man in an illusory way.   In politics, the Germans have *thought* what other nations have *done*.   Germany has been their *theoretical consciousness*.   The abstraction and presumption of its philosophy was in step with the partial and stunted character of their reality.   If, therefore, the *status quo* of the *German political system* expresses the *consummation of the ancien régime*, the thorn in the flesh of the modern state, the *status quo* of

German political science expresses the *imperfection of the modern state* itself, the degeneracy of its flesh.

As the determined adversary of the previous form of German political consciousness, the criticism of the speculative philosophy of right does not remain within its own sphere, but leads on to *tasks* which can only be solved by *means of practical activity*.

The question then arises: can Germany attain a practical activity *à la hauteur des principes*; that is to say, a revolution which will raise it not only to the *official level* of the modern nations, but to the *human level* which will be the immediate future of those nations.

It is clear that the arm of criticism cannot replace the criticism of arms. Material force can only be overthrown by material force; but theory itself becomes a material force when it has seized the masses. Theory is capable of seizing the masses when it demonstrates *ad hominem*, and it demonstrates *ad hominem* as soon as it becomes radical. To be radical is to grasp things by the root. But for man the root is man himself. What proves beyond doubt the radicalism of Germany theory, and thus its practical energy, is that it begins from the resolute *positive* abolition of religion. The criticism of religion ends with the doctrine that *man is the supreme being for man*. It ends, therefore, with the *categorical imperative to overthrow all those conditions* in which man is an abased, enslaved, abandoned, contemptible being—conditions which can hardly be better described than in the exclamation of a Frenchman on the occasion of a proposed tax upon dogs: " Wretched dogs! They want to treat you like men! "

Even from the historical standpoint theoretical emancipation has a specific practical importance for Germany. In fact Germany's *revolutionary* past is theoretical—it is the *Reformation*. In that period the revolution originated in the brain of a monk, today in the brain of the philosopher.

Luther, without question, overcame servitude through

devotion but only by substituting servitude through *conviction*. He shattered the faith in authority by restoring the authority of faith. He transformed the priests into laymen by turning laymen into priests. He liberated man from external religiosity by making religiosity the innermost essence of man. He liberated the body from its chains because he fettered the heart with chains.

But if Protestantism was not the solution it did at least pose the problem correctly. It was no longer a question, thereafter, of the layman's struggle against the priest outside himself, but of his struggle against his *own internal priest*, against his own *priestly nature*. And if the Protestant metamorphosis of German laymen into priests emancipated the lay popes—the *princes* together with their clergy, the privileged and the philistines—the philosophical metamorphosis of the priestly Germans into men will emancipate the *people*. But just as emancipation will not be confined to princes, so the *secularization* of property will not be limited to the *confiscation of church property*, which was practised especially by hypocritical Prussia. At that time, the Peasant War, the most radical event in German history, came to grief because of theology.

Today, when theology itself has come to grief, the most unfree phenomenon in German history—our *status quo*—will be shattered by philosophy. On the eve of the Reformation official Germany was the most abject servant of Rome. On the eve of its revolution Germany is the abject servant of those who are far inferior to Rome; of Prussia and Austria, of petty squires and philistines.

But a *radical* revolution in Germany seems to encounter a major difficulty.

Revolutions need a *passive* element, a *material* basis. Theory is only realized in a people so far as it fulfils the needs of the people. Will there correspond to the monstrous discrepancy between the demands of German thought and the answers of German reality a similar discrepancy between civil society and the state, and within civil society itself?

Will theoretical needs be directly practical needs? It is not enough that thought should seek to realize itself; reality must also strive towards thought.

But Germany has not passed through the intermediate stage of political emancipation at the same time as the modern nations. It has not yet attained in practice those stages which it has transcended in theory. How could Germany, in *salta mortale*, surmount not only its own barriers but also those of the modern nations, that is, those barriers which it must in reality experience and strive for as an emancipation from its own real barriers? A radical revolution can only be a revolution of radical needs, for which the conditions and breeding ground appear to be lacking.

But if Germany accompanied the development of the modern nations only through the abstract activity of thought, without taking an active part in the real struggles of this development, it has also experienced the *pains* of this development without sharing in its pleasures and partial satisfactions. The abstract activity on one side has its counterpart in the abstract suffering on the other. And one fine day Germany will find itself at the level of the European decadence, before ever having attained the level of European emancipation. It will be comparable to a fetishist who is sickening from the diseases of Christianity.

If the *German governments* are examined it will be found that the circumstances of the time, the situation of Germany, the outlook of German culture, and lastly their own fortunate instinct, all drive them to combine the *civilized deficiencies* of the *modern political world* (whose advantages we do not enjoy) with the *barbarous deficiencies* of the *ancien régime* (which we enjoy in full measure); so that Germany must participate more and more, if not in the reason at least in the unreason of those political systems which transcend its *status quo*. Is there, for example, any country in the whole world which shares with such naïveté as so-called constitutional Germany all the illusions of the constitutional régime without sharing its realities? And was it not, of necessity, a German government which had the idea of combining the torments of censorship with the torments of the French September laws [1] which presuppose the liberty of the Press? Just as the gods of all the nations were to be found in the Roman Pantheon, so there will be found in the Holy Roman German Empire all the *sins* of all the forms of State. That this eclecticism will attain an unprecedented degree is assured in particular by the *politico-aesthetic gourmandise* of a German king who proposes to play all the roles of royalty—feudal or bureaucratic, absolute or constitutional, autocratic or democratic—if not in the person of the people at least in his *own* person, and if not for the people, at least for *himself*. *Germany, as the deficiency of present-day politics constituted into a system*, will not be able to demolish the specific German barriers without demolishing the general barriers of present-day politics.

It is not *radical* revolution, *universal human* emancipation, which is a Utopian dream for Germany, but rather a partial, *merely* political revolution which leaves the pillars of the building standing. What is the basis of a partial, merely political revolution? Simply this: a *section of civil society* emancipates itself and attains universal domination; a determinate class undertakes, from its *particular situation*, a general emancipation of society. This class emancipates society as a whole, but only on condition that the whole of society is in the same situation as this class; for example, that it possesses or can easily acquire money or culture.

No class in civil society can play this part unless it can arouse, in itself and in the masses, a moment of enthusiasm in which it associates and mingles with society at large, identifies itself with it, and is felt and recognized as the *general representative* of this society. Its aims and interests must genuinely

---

[1] The laws of September 1835 which increased the financial guarantees required from the publishers of newspapers and introduced heavier penalties for " subversive " publications. [*Editor's note.*]

be the aims and interests of society itself, of which it becomes in reality the social head and heart. It is only in the name of general interests that a particular class can claim general supremacy. In order to attain this liberating position, and the political direction of all spheres of society, revolutionary energy and consciousness of its own power do not suffice. For a *popular revolution* and the *emancipation of a particular class* of civil society to coincide, for *one* class to represent the whole of society, another class must concentrate in itself all the evils of society, a particular class must embody and represent a general obstacle and limitation. A particular social sphere must be regarded as the *notorious crime* of the whole society, so that emancipation from this sphere appears as a general emancipation. For *one* class to be the liberating class *par excellence*, it is necessary that another class should be openly the oppressing class. The negative significance of the French nobility and clergy produced the positive significance of the bourgeoisie, the class which stood next to them and opposed them.

But in Germany every class lacks the logic, insight, courage and clarity which would make it a negative representative of society. Moreover, there is also lacking in every class the generosity of spirit which identifies itself, if only for a moment, with the popular mind; that genius which pushes material force to political power, that revolutionary daring which throws at its adversary the defiant phrase: *I am nothing and I should be everything*. The essence of German morality and honour, in classes as in individuals, is a *modest egoism* which displays, and allows others to display, its own narrowness. The relation between the different spheres of German society is, therefore, not dramatic, but epic. Each of these spheres begins to be aware of itself and to establish itself beside the others, not from the moment when it is oppressed, but from the moment that circumstances, without any action of its own, have created a new sphere which it can in turn oppress. Even the *moral sentiment of the German middle class* has no other basis than the consciousness of being the representative of the narrow and limited mediocrity of all the other classes.   It is not only the German kings, therefore, who ascend their thrones *mal à propos*.   Each sphere of civil society suffers a defeat before gaining the victory; it erects its own barrier before having destroyed the barrier which opposes it; it displays the narrowness of its views before having displayed their generosity, and thus every opportunity of playing an important role has passed before it properly existed, and each class, at the very moment when it begins its struggle against the class above it, remains involved in a struggle against the class beneath.   For this reason, the princes are in conflict with the monarch, the bureaucracy with the nobility, the bourgeoisie with all of them, while the proletariat is already beginning its struggle with the bourgeoisie.   The middle class hardly dares to conceive the idea of emancipation from its own point of view before the development of social conditions, and the progress of political theory, show that this point of view is already antiquated, or at least disputable.

In France it is enough to be something in order to desire to be everything.   In Germany no one has the right to be anything without first renouncing everything.   In France partial emancipation is a basis for complete emancipation.   In Germany complet emancipation is a *conditio sine qua non* for any partial emancipation.   In France it is the reality, in Germany the impossibility, of a progressive emancipation which must give birth to complete liberty.   In France every class of the population is *politically idealistic* and considers itself first of all, not as a particular class, but as the representative of the general needs of society.   The role of liberator can, therefore, pass successively in a dramatic movement to different classes in the population, until it finally reaches the class which achieves social freedom;   no longer assuming certain conditions external to man, which are none the less created by human society, but organizing all the conditions of human life on the basis of social freedom. In Germany, on the contrary, where practical life is as little intellectual as intellectual life is practical, no class of civil society feels the need for, or the ability to achieve, a general emancipation, until it is forced to it by its *immediate* situation, by *material* necessity and by its *fetters themselves*.

Where is there, then, a *real* possibility of emancipation in Germany?

This is our reply. A class must be formed which has *radical chains*, a class in civil society which is not a class of civil society, a class which is the dissolution of all classes, a sphere of society which has a universal character because its sufferings are universal, and which does not claim a *particular redress* because the wrong which is done to it is not a *particular wrong* but *wrong in general*. There must be formed a sphere of society which claims no *traditional* status but only a human status, a sphere which is not opposed to particular consequences but is totally opposed to the assumptions of the German political system; a sphere, finally, which cannot emancipate itself without emancipating itself from all the other spheres of society, without, therefore, emancipating all these other spheres, which is, in short, a *total loss* of humanity and which can only redeem itself by a *total redemption of humanity*. This dissolution of society, as a particular class, is the *proletariat*.

The proletariat is only beginning to form itself in Germany, as a result of the industrial movement. For what constitutes the proletariat is not *naturally existing* poverty, but poverty *artificially produced*, is not the mass of people mechanically oppressed by the weight of society, but the mass resulting from the *disintegration* of society and above all from the disintegration of the middle class. Needless to say, however, the numbers of the proletariat are also increased by the victims of natural poverty and of Christian-Germanic serfdom.

When the proletariat announces the *dissolution of the existing social order*, it only declares the *secret of its* own existence, for it *is* the *effective* dissolution of this order.   When the proletariat demands the *negation of private property* it only lays down as a *principle for society* what society has already made a principle *for the proletariat*, and what the *latter* already involuntarily embodies as the negative result of society.   Thus the proletarian has the same right, in relation to the new world which is coming into being, as the *German king* has in relation to the existing world when he calls the people *his* people or a horse *his* horse.   In calling the people his private property the king simply declares that the owner of private property is king.

Just as philosophy finds its *material* weapons in the proletariat, so the proletariat finds its *intellectual* weapons in philosophy.   And once the lightning of thought has penetrated deeply into this virgin soil of the people, the *Germans* will emancipate themselves and become *men*.

Let us sum up these results.   The emancipation of Germany is only possible *in practice* if one adopts the point of view of that theory according to which man is the highest being for man.   Germany will not be able to emancipate itself from the *Middle Ages* unless it emancipates itself at the same time from the *partial* victories over the Middle Ages. In Germany *no* type of enslavement can be abolished unless *all* enslavement is destroyed.   Germany, which likes to get to the bottom of things, can only make a revolution which upsets *the whole order* of things.   The *emancipation of Germany* will be an *emancipation of man*.   *Philosophy* is the *head* of this emancipation and the *proletariat* is its *heart*.   Philosophy can only be realized by the abolition of the proletariat, and the proletariat can only be abolished by the realization of philosophy.

ECONOMIC AND PHILOSOPHICAL
MANUSCRIPTS

PREFACE [1]

(from the Third Manuscript)

I HAVE already announced in the *Deutsch-Französische Jahrbücher* [2] a forthcoming critique of jurisprudence and political science in the form of a critique of the *Hegelian* philosophy of right. However, in preparing the work for publication it became apparent that a combination of the criticism directed solely against the speculative theory with the criticism of the various subjects would be quite unsuitable; it would hamper the development of the argument and make it more difficult to follow. Moreover, I could only have compressed such a wealth of diverse subjects into a *single* work by writing in an aphoristic style, and such an aphoristic presentation would have given the *impression* of arbitrary systematization. I shall, therefore, publish my critique of law, morals, politics, etc. in a number of independent brochures; and finally I shall endeavour, in a separate work, to present the interconnected whole, to show the relationships between the parts, and to provide a critique of the speculative treatment of this material. That is why, in the present work, the relationships of political economy with the state, law, morals, civil life, etc. are touched upon only to the extent that political economy itself expressly deals with these subjects.

It is hardly necessary to assure the reader who is familiar with political economy that my conclusions are the fruit of an entirely empirical analysis, based upon a careful critical study of political economy.

It goes without saying that in addition to the French and

---

[1] I have not included the few passages which Marx deleted in the manuscript. They add nothing of interest to the text. [*Editor's note.*]

[2] Marx refers to his essay " Zur Kritik der Hegelschen Rechtsphilosophie," which is translated in the present volume, pp. 43–59 above. [*Editor's note.*]

English socialists I have also used German socialist writings. But the *original* and important German works on this subject —apart from the writings of Weitling—are limited to the essays published by Hess in the *Einundzwanzig Bogen*,[1] and Engels' " Umrisse zur [2] Kritik des Nationalökonomie " in the *Deutsch-Französische Jahrbücher*.[3] In the latter publication I myself have indicated in a very general way the basic elements of the present work.[4]

The *positive*, humanistic and naturalistic criticism begins with Feuerbach. The less blatant Feuerbach's writings, the more certain, profound, extensive and lasting is their influence; they are the only writings since Hegel's *Phenomenology* and *Logic* which contain a real theoretical revolution.

Unlike the *critical theologians* of our time I have considered that a critical exposition of the *Hegelian dialectic* and general philosophy, which forms the final chapter of the present work, is absolutely essential, for the task has not yet been accomplished. This *lack of thoroughness* is not accidental, for the *critical* theologian remains a *theologian*. He must either begin from certain presuppositions of philosophy accepted as authoritative, or, if doubts have arisen in his mind concerning the philosophical presuppositions in the course of criticism and as a result of other people's discoveries, he abandons them in a cowardly and unjustified manner, *abstracts* from them, and shows both his servile dependence upon them and his resentment of this dependence in a negative, unconscious and sophistical way.

Looked at more closely, *theological criticism*, which was at the beginning of the movement a genuinely progressive factor, is seen to be, in the last analysis, no more than the

---

[1] *Einundzwanzig Bogen aus der Schweiz*, edited by Georg Herwegh. First part, Zürich and Winterthur, 1843. Marx refers to the articles by Hess: " Sozialismus und Kommunismus," pp. 79–91; " Die eine und ganze Freiheit," pp. 92–7; " Philosophie der Tat," pp. 309–31. [*Editor's note.*]

[2] This should read *zu einer*. [*Editor's note.*]

[3] *Deutsch-Französische Jahrbücher*, pp. 86–114.

[4] See note 1 on p. 44 above. [*Editor's note.*]

culmination and consequence of the old *philosophical*, and especially *Hegelian*, *transcendentalism* distorted into a *theological caricature*. I shall describe elsewhere, at greater length, this interesting act of historical justice, this Nemesis which now destines theology, ever the infected spot of philosophy, to portray in itself the negative dissolution of philosophy, i.e. the process of its decay.

FIRST MANUSCRIPT

WAGES OF LABOUR

[I] *Wages* are determined by the bitter struggle between capitalist and worker. The necessary victory of the capitalist. The capitalist can live longer without the worker than can the worker without the capitalist. Combination among capitalists is usual and effective, whereas combination among workers is proscribed and has painful consequences for them. Moreover, the landowner and capitalist can supplement their revenues with the profits of industry, while the worker has neither ground rent nor interest on capital to add to his industrial earnings. Hence, the intensity of competition among workers. Only for the workers, therefore, is the separation of capital, landed property and labour an inescapable, vital and harmful separation. Capital and landed property need not remain in this abstraction, as must the labour of the workers.

For the worker, therefore, the separation of capital, ground rent and labour is fatal.

The lowest and the only necessary rate of wages is that which provides for the subsistence of the worker during work and for a supplement adequate to raise a family so that the race of workers does not die out. According to Smith, the normal wage is the lowest which is compatible with common humanity [1] that is, with a bestial existence.

The demand for men necessarily regulates the production of men, as of every other commodity. If the supply greatly exceeds the demand, then a section of the workers declines into beggary or starvation. Thus, the existence of the worker is reduced to the same conditions as the existence of any other commodity. The worker has become a commodity and he is

---

[1] ADAM SMITH, *The Wealth of Nations* (2 vols. Everyman edition) I, p. 61. Marx quotes from the French translation: *Recherches sur la nature et les causes de la richesse des nations*; par Adam Smith. Traduction nouvelle, avec les notes et observations; par Germain Garnier. T. I–IV. Paris, 1802.

fortunate if he can find a buyer. And the demand, upon which the worker's life depends, is determined by the caprice of the wealthy and the capitalists. If the supply exceeds the demand, one of the elements entering into price—profit, ground rent, wages—will be paid below its *rate*; a part of the supply of these factors will then be withdrawn from this use and the market price will gravitate towards the natural price. But (1) where there is an extensive division of labour it is extremely difficult for the worker to direct his labour into other uses, and (2) because of his subordination to the capitalist, he is the first to suffer hardship.

The worker, therefore, loses most, and loses inevitably, from the gravitation of the market price to the natural price. At the same time, it is the ability of the capitalist to put his capital to other uses which either condemns the worker, who is limited to one employment of his labour, to starvation or forces him to accept every demand which the capitalist makes.

[II] The adventitious and sudden variations in market price affect ground rent less than those parts of the price which comprise profit and wages, but they affect profit less than wages. In most cases, for every wage which rises there is one which remains *stationary* and one which *falls*.

The worker does not necessarily gain when the capitalist gains, but he necessarily loses with him. Thus, the worker does not gain if the capitalist succeeds in maintaining the market price above the natural price by means of a manufacturing or commercial secret, a monopoly or the favourable situation of his property.

Further, *the prices of labour are much more stable than the prices of provisions.* They often vary inversely. In a dear year, wages fall, because of the decline in demand, but rise because of the increase in the price of provisions; so they balance. In any event, numbers of workers are without bread. In cheap years, wages rise because of increased demand, and fall because of the low prices of provisions; so they balance.[1]

---

[1] SMITH, I, pp. 76–7.

Another disadvantage of the worker: *The wage rates of different kinds of workers vary much more than do the profits in the different branches in which capital is employed.* In work, all the natural, spiritual and social differences of individual activity appear and are differently remunerated, while dead capital maintains an unvarying performance and is indifferent to *real* individual activity.

In general, it should be noted that where worker and capitalist both suffer, the worker suffers in his existence while the capitalist suffers in the profit on his dead mammon.

The worker has not only to struggle for his physical means of subsistence; he must also struggle to obtain work, i.e. for the possibility and the means to perform his activity. Let us take three conditions in which society may find itself, and consider the situation of the worker in each of them.[1]

1. If the wealth of society is diminishing, the worker suffers most, for although the working class cannot gain as much as the class of property owners in a prosperous state of society, *none suffers so cruelly from its decline as the working class*.[2]

[III] 2. Let us next take a society in which wealth is increasing. This situation is the only one favourable to the worker. In this case, there is competition among capitalists and the demand for workers exceeds the supply. But, *in the first place*, the raising of wages leads to *overwork* among the workers. The more they want to earn the more they must sacrifice their time and perform slave labour in which their freedom is totally alienated in the service of avarice. In so doing they shorten their lives. This shortening of the life span is a favourable circumstance for the working class as a whole, since it makes necessary an ever renewed supply of workers. This class must always sacrifice a part of itself, in order not to be uined as a whole.

[1] SMITH, I, pp. 61–5. [2] Ibid., p. 230.

Furthermore, when is a society in a condition of increasing wealth? When the capital and revenues of a country are growing. But this is only possible (α) when much labour is accumulated, for capital is accumulated labour; when, therefore, more of the worker's product is taken from him, when his own labour becomes opposed to him as an alien possession, and when his means of existence and his activity are increasingly concentrated in the hands of the capitalist. (β) The accumulation of capital increases the division of labour, and the division of labour increases the number of workers; conversely, the increasing number of workers increases the division of labour, and the increasing division of labour increases the accumulation of capital. As a result of the division of labour on one hand, and the accumulation of capital on the other hand, the worker becomes even more completely dependent upon labour, and upon a particular, extremely one-sided, mechanical kind of labour. Just as he is reduced, therefore, both spiritually and physically to the condition of a machine, and from being a man becomes merely an abstract activity and a belly, so he becomes increasingly dependent upon all the fluctuations in market price, in the employment of capital, and in the caprices of the rich. Equally, the growth of the class of men who are [IV] entirely dependent upon work increases competition among the workers and lowers their price. In the factory system this situation of the workers reaches its climax.

(γ) In a society where prosperity is increasing, only the very wealthiest can live from the interest on money. All others must employ their capital in business or trade. As a result the competition among capitalists increases. The concentration of capital becomes greater, the large capitalists ruin the small ones, and some of the former capitalists sink into the working class which, as a result of this accession of numbers, suffers a further decline in wages and falls into still greater dependence upon the few great capitalists. Since, at the same time, the number of capitalists has diminished, the competition among them for workers hardly exists any longer, whereas the competition among workers, on account of the increase in their numbers, has become greater, more abnormal and more violent. Consequently, a part of the working class falls into a condition of beggary or starvation, with the same necessity as a section of the middle capitalists falls into the working class.

Thus, even in the state of society which is most favourable to the worker, the inevitable result for the worker is overwork and premature death, reduction to a machine, enslavement to capital which accumulates in menacing opposition to him, renewed competition, and beggary or starvation for a part of the workers.

[V] Rising wages awake in the worker the same desire for enrichment as in the capitalist, but he can only satisfy it by the sacrifice of his body and spirit. Rising wages presuppose, and also bring about, the accumulation of capital; thus they increasingly alienate the product of labour from the worker. Likewise, the division of labour makes him increasingly one-sided and dependent, and introduces competition not only from other men but also from machines. Since the worker has been reduced to a machine, the machine can compete with him. Finally, just as the accumulation of capital increases the amount of industry, and thus the number of workers, so as a result of this accumulation the same volume of industry produces a *greater quantity of products* which leads to overproduction and culminates either in putting a great part of the workers out of work or in reducing their wages to the most wretched minimum. Such are the consequences of a state of society which is most favourable to the worker, namely a state of increasing, developing wealth.

Eventually, however, this state of growth must reach its culmination. What is then the condition of the worker?

3. " In a country which had acquired that full complement of riches . . . both the wages of labour and the profits of stock would probably be very low . . . the competition for employment would necessarily be so great as to reduce the wages of labour to what was barely sufficient to keep up the number of labourers, and, the country being already fully peopled, that number could never be augmented." [1] The excess would have to die.

Thus, in a declining state of society, increasing misery of the worker; in a progressive state, complicated misery; and in the final state, stationary misery.

[VI] Since, however, according to Smith a society is not happy in which the majority suffers, and since the wealthiest state of society leads to suffering for the majority, while the economic system (in general, a society of private interests) leads to this wealthiest state, it follows that social *misery* is the goal of the economy.

It should be noted in connexion with the relation between worker and capitalist that the capitalist is more than compensated for wage increases by the reduction of working time, and that wage increases and increases in the interest on capital affect the price of commodities in the manner of simple and compound interest.

Let us now adopt entirely the viewpoint of the economist and compare in his terms the theoretical and practical claims of the workers.

He tells us that originally, and in principle, the *whole product* of labour belongs to the worker. But he adds immediately that, in fact, the worker receives only the smallest and absolutely indispensable part of the product; just so much as is necessary for him to exist as a worker, not as a human being, and for him to engender the slave class of workers, not humanity.

The economist tells us that everything is bought with

[1] Smith, I, p. 84.

labour, and that capital is only accumulated labour, but he adds immediately that the worker, far from being able to buy everything must sell himself and his human qualities.

While the ground rent of the idle landowner usually amounts to one-third of the produce of the land, and the profit of the busy capitalist amounts to double the rate of interest, the surplus which the worker earns in the most favourable case is so little that two of his four children are condemned to die of hunger.[1] [VII] Whereas according to the economists, it is through labour alone that man increases the value of natural products, and labour is man's active property; yet according to this same political economy the landowner and the capitalist, who as such are merely privileged and idle gods, are everywhere raised above the worker and prescribe laws for him.

According to the economists labour is the only unchanging price of things, yet nothing is more fortuitous nor subject to greater fluctuations than the price of labour.

Although the division of labour increases the productive power of labour and the wealth and refinement of society, it impoverishes the worker and makes him into a machine. Although labour promotes the accumulation of capital and thus the growing prosperity of society, it makes the worker increasingly dependent upon the capitalist, exposes him to greater competition, and drives him into the hectic course of overproduction followed by a corresponding slump.

Although, according to the economists, the interest of the worker is never opposed to the interest of society, society is always and necessarily opposed to the interest of the worker.

According to the economists the interest of the worker is never opposed to that of society (1) because the increase of wages is more than compensated by the reduction of working time, with the other consequences discussed earlier, and (2) because in relation to society the whole gross product is

[1] SMITH, I, p. 60.

net product, and net product only has meaning for the private individual.

I maintain, however, that labour itself, not only in present conditions but universally in so far as its purpose is merely the increase of wealth, is harmful and deleterious, and that this conclusion follows from the economist's own argument, though he is unaware of it.

In theory, rent and profit are *deductions* which wages have to bear. In reality, however, wages are a deduction which land and capital allow to the worker, a concession made by the product of labour to the worker, to labour.

In the declining state of society, the worker suffers most. The particular severity of his hardship is due to his situation as a worker, but the hardship in general is due to the condition of society.

In the progressive state of society, however, the decline and impoverishment of the worker is the product of his own labour and of the wealth produced by him. Misery, therefore, emerges spontaneously out of the essence of present-day labour.

The most opulent state of society, which is an ideal, yet one which is gradually approached and which is at least the aim of political economy and of civil society, is a state of *stationary misery* for the workers.

It is self-evident that political economy treats the *proletarian*, i.e. one who lives, without capital or rent, simply from labour, and from one-sided, abstract labour, merely as a *worker*. It can, therefore, propound the thesis that he, like a horse, must receive just as much as will enable him to work. Political economy does not deal with him in his free time, as a human being, but leaves this aspect to the criminal law, doctors, religion, statistical tables, politics and the workhouse beadle.

Let us now rise above the level of political economy and

seek from the foregoing argument, which was presented almost in the words of the economists, answers to two questions—

1. What is the significance, in the development of mankind, of this reduction of the greater part of mankind to abstract labour?

2. What errors are committed by the advocates of piecemeal reform, who either want to raise wages and thereby improve the condition of the working class, or (like Proudhon) regard *equality* of wages as the aim of the social revolution?

In political economy *labour* appears only in the form of *acquisitive activity.*

[VIII] " It may be argued that those occupations which call for specific aptitudes or a longer training, have become, on the whole, more remunerative, while the wages for mechanical, uniform activity, which anyone can be taught quickly and easily, have fallen and must necessarily fall as a result of competition. And it is just *this* kind of labour which, in the present state of the organization of work, is the most common. If a worker in the first category now earns seven times as much, and one in the second category just as much as fifty years ago, then certainly the *average* earnings of the two together are now four times as much. But if, in a particular country, only one thousand people are occupied in the first category, and one million in the second, then 999,000 are no better off than fifty years earlier; and indeed they are *worse off* if the prices of the necessaries of life have risen. And yet it is with such superficial *average* calculations that one deceives, or tries to deceive, oneself about the condition of the most numerous class of the population. In addition, wage *rates* are only *one* element affecting the *incomes* of workers, for it is necessary to take into account also the guaranteed *duration* of work, and there can be no question of this in the anarchic system of free competition with its

ever-recurring recessions and stagnation. Finally we must
take into account the normal *hours of work* at the present time
and in the past. For the English workers in the cotton
industry these have risen to twelve to sixteen hours a day in
the past twenty-five years, i.e. precisely since the introduction of labour-saving machinery, through the acquisitiveness
of the entrepreneurs.

[IX] This increase in one country and in one branch of
industry must, according to the well-recognized rights of
unlimited exploitation of the poor by the rich, become more
or less established elsewhere." [1]

" Even if it were as true, as it is in fact false, that the
average incomes of *all* classes of society had increased, the
disparity of incomes could still have increased, and thus the
contrast between wealth and poverty could have appeared
more clearly. For it is *because* total production increases,
and in the same measure, that needs, desires and wants also
increase, and *relative* poverty may grow while *absolute* poverty
diminishes. The Samoyed is not poor with his blubber and
rancid fish, because in *his* isolated society everyone has the
same needs. But in a *developing* society, which in the course
of a decade increases its total production in relation to the
population by one-third, the worker who earns the same
amount at the end of ten years has not remained as well off
as he was, but has become more needy by a third." [2]

---

[1] WILHELM SCHULZ, *Die Bewegung der Produktion, Eine geschichtlich-statistiche
Abhandlung.* Zürich and Winterthur, 1843, p. 65. Marx quotes this passage
with minor omissions. [*Editor's note.*]

[2] Ibid., pp. 65–6. Marx himself used the same argument later in discussing
the "increasing misery of the working class," even in the most favourable
condition of society when wages are increasing: "An appreciable rise in
wages presupposes a rapid growth of productive capital. Rapid growth of
productive capital calls forth just as rapid a growth of wealth, of luxury, of
social needs and social pleasures. Therefore, although the pleasures of the
labourer have increased, the social gratification which they afford has fallen
in comparison with the increased pleasures of the capitalist, which are in-
accessible to the worker, in comparison with the stage of development of
society in general. Our wants and pleasures have their origin in society; we
therefore measure them in relation to society; we do not measure them in relation to the objects which serve for their gratification. Since they are of a social

But political economy conceives the worker only as a draught animal, as a beast whose needs are strictly limited to bodily needs.

" A nation which aims to develop its culture more freely can no longer remain the slave of its material needs, the bondsman of its body. It needs above all leisure *time* in which to produce and to enjoy culture. The progress of the organization of work creates this leisure. A single worker in the cotton industry now often produces, with the aid of new sources of power and improved machines, as much as 100, or even 250–350 workers produced formerly. There are similar achievements even if not on the same scale in all branches of production, as a necessary consequence of the fact that the forces of nature are more and more forced into collaboration [X] with human labour. If the amount of time and human effort which was needed at an earlier date, in order to satisfy a given sum of material needs, has been reduced by half, then the time available for cultural creation and enjoyment, without any diminution in material well-being, has increased by the same amount. . . . But the division of the spoils which we take from Father Time on his own ground is still determined by blind and inequitable chance. It has been calculated that in France, at the present level of production, an average of five hours' work daily from each person able to work would suffice to meet all the material needs of society . . . in spite of the saving of time through the improvements in machinery the duration of slave labour in factories has increased for a large number of people." [1]

" The transition from complex craftmanship presupposes that the work is divided into simple operations. But only *a part* of the uniform, repetitive operations is performed by

nature, they are of a relative nature." *Wage-Labour and Capital* (Lectures delivered to the German Workingmen's Club of Brussels in 1847, and first published as a series of leading articles in the *Neue Rheinische Zeitung* from 4th April, 1849). [*Editor's note.*]

[1] Op. cit., pp. 67–8. Quoted with minor omissions. [*Editor's note.*]

the machines, another part by men. Such continued, uniform work is, by its nature (and this is confirmed by investigation), harmful to the spirit no less than to the body; and when the use of machinery is *associated* with the division of labour among large numbers of men all the disadvantages of the latter make their appearance. These disadvantages are revealed, for example, by the high mortality of factory [XI] workers. . . . [1] The important distinction between how far men work *with* machines or *as* machines, has not received attention. . . . [2] "

" But in the future life of mankind, the mindless forces of nature at work in machinery will be our slaves and serfs." [3]

" In the English cotton spinning mills only 158,818 men are employed as against 196,818 women. For every 100 male workers in the Lancashire cotton mills there are 103 women workers, and in Scotland 209 women for every 100 men. In the English flax factories in Leeds there were 147 women for every 100 male workers; in Dundee and on the East coast of Scotland, 280 women for every 100 men. In the English silk factories . . . many women workers; in the wool factories, which require greater physical strength, there are more men . . . Likewise, in the North American cotton mills, in 1833, there were 38,927 women employed along with 18,593 men. Thus, the changes in the organization of work have brought a wider sphere of gainful activity for women . . . a more independent economic situation for married women . . . and closer social relationships between the sexes." [4]

" In the English cotton spinning mills operated by water and steam power, there were employed in 1835: 20,558 children between 8–12 years of age; 35,867 between 12–13; and 108,208 between 13–18 . . . It is true that the progress of

---

[1] This sentence comes from a footnote in the original. [*Editor's note.*]
[2] Ibid., p. 69.
[3] Ibid., p. 74.   [4] Ibid., pp. 71–2.

machinery, in so far as it removes all uniform operations more and more from human hands, tends towards a complete elimination [XII] of these evils. But there stands in the way of such rapid progress the fact that the capitalists can acquire the labour of the lower classes, even of children, very easily and cheaply, and use it *instead* of making use of machinery." [1]

" Lord Brougham's appeal to the workers: ' Become capitalists! ' . . . the evil that millions of men are only able to gain a bare living by exhausting, physically injurious, and morally and spiritually crippling labour; that they must even consider themselves fortunate to have the misfortune to find *such* work." [2]

" In order to live, therefore, the non-owners are obliged to put themselves directly or indirectly in the service of the owners, i.e. to become their dependants." [3]

" Domestic servants—wages (*gages*); workers—wages (*salaires*); clerks—salaries or emoluments (*traitements ou émoluments*)." [4]

. . . " hire out one's labour," " lend one's labour at interest," " work in place of someone else."

. . . " hire out the materials of labour," " lend the materials of labour at interest," " make someone else work in one's place." [5]

[XIII] " This economic order condemns men to such abject occupations, to such desolate and bitter degradation, that by comparison savagery appears a royal condition." [6] " Prostitution of the non-owning class in every respect." [7] Ragpicker.

Ch. Loudon, in the work *Solution du problème de la population,*

[1] Op. cit., pp. 70–1.
[2] Ibid., p. 60.
[3] C. PECQUEUR, *Théorie nouvelle d'économie sociale et politique, ou études sur l'organisation des sociétés.* Paris 1842, p. 409.
[4] Ibid., pp. 409–10.
[5] Ibid., p. 411.
[6] Ibid., pp. 417–18.
[7] Ibid., pp. 421 *et seq.*

Paris 1842,[1] gives the number of prostitutes in England as 60–70,000. The number of women of " doubtful virtue " is about the same.[2]

" The average life of these unfortunate creatures on the streets, after they have entered the career of vice, is about six or seven years. So that in order to maintain the number of 60–70,000 prostitutes, there must be at least 8–9,000 women, in the three kingdoms, who adopt this infamous trade each year; that is, about twenty-four new victims every day, or an average of *one* every hour. Thus, if the same proportion holds throughout the world, there must constantly be one and a half million of these miserable beings." [3]

" . . . the numbers of the poor increase with their poverty, and it is in the most extreme state of want that human beings crowd in the greatest number to contend for the right to suffer. . . . In 1821, the population of Ireland was 6,801,827. In 1831, it had risen to 7,764,010; an increase of fourteen per cent in ten years. In Leinster, a province where there is least poverty, the population increased only by eight per cent, whereas in Connaught, the poorest province, the increase attained twenty-one per cent (*Extract from Reports on Ireland published in England*, Vienna 1840)." [4] Political economy considers labour abstractly as a thing. Labour is a commodity; if the price is high the demand is great, and if the price is low the supply is great. As with other commodities, the price of labour must diminish; it is partly the competition between capitalist and worker, partly the competition among workers themselves, which brings this about. " The working population, seller of labour, is necessarily

---

[1] CHARLES LOUDON, *Solution du problème de la population et de la subsistance, soumise à un médecin dans une série de lettres*, Paris, 1842.

[2] Ibid., p. 228. Loudon gives these figures for the " three kingdoms," i.e. for the United Kingdom, not for England alone. [*Editor's note.*]

[3] Ibid., p. 229.

[4] EUGÈNE BURET, *De la misère des classes laborieuses en Angleterre et en France.* T. I–II. Paris, 1840. I., pp. 36–7. The latter part of this quotation is from footnote 1 to p. 36. [*Editor's note.*]

reduced to the smallest part of the product. . . . Is the theory of labour as a commodity anything but a disguised theory of servitude? " [1] " Why was labour regarded only as an exchange value? " [2] The large factories prefer to buy the labour of women and children, because it is cheaper than that of men.   " The worker, *vis-à-vis* his employer is not at all in the situation of *someone who sells freely* . . . the capitalist is always free to employ labour, and the worker is always obliged to sell it.   The value of labour is completely destroyed, if it is not sold at every instant.   Labour can neither be accumulated nor saved, unlike genuine commodities. [XIV] Labour is life, and if life is not exchanged every day for food it soon suffers and perishes.   If the life of man is to be a commodity, then slavery must be acknowledged." [3] Thus, if labour is a commodity, it is a commodity of the most wretched kind.   But even according to economic principles, it is not a commodity, since it is not the *free product of a free market*.   The present economic system " reduces at the same time the price and the reward of labour, it perfects the worker and degrades the man." [4]   " Industry has become a war, and commerce a game." [5]

The cotton-spinning machines (in England) were equivalent to 84,000,000 handworkers.

Industry has been up to now in the situation of a war of conquest; " it has expended the lives of those who composed its army with the same indifference as the great conquerors. Its aim was the possession of wealth, not the happiness of mankind." [6]   " These interests [i.e. economic interests] if left entirely to themselves . . . must necessarily enter into conflict; they have no other arbiter but war, and the decisions of war assign defeat and death to one side and victory to the other . . . it is in the conflict of opposed forces that science looks for order and equilibrium: *perpetual war* is, in

---

[1] BURET, op. cit., p. 43.   [2] Ibid., p. 44.
[3] Ibid., pp. 49–50.   Emphasis added by Marx.   [*Editor's note.*]
[4] Ibid., pp. 52–3.   [5] Ibid., p. 62.   [6] Ibid., p. 20.

its view, the only way of obtaining peace; this war is called competition." [1]

" The industrial war, in order to produce results, requires very large armies which can be concentrated upon one point and sacrificed without restraint. The soldiers of this army support the burdens which are placed upon them neither from devotion nor from duty, but only to escape the hard fate of hunger. They have neither affection nor gratitude for their chiefs; the latter are not bound to their subordinates by any feeling of goodwill, and regard them not as men but as instruments of production which must yield as much as possible and cost as little as possible. These herds of workers, ever more crowded together, do not even have the assurance that they will always be employed. Industry, which has called them together, only allows them to live when it needs them; as soon as it can dispense with them, it abandons them without the slightest concern. Then the workers who have been dismissed are obliged to offer their bodies and their labour for whatever price is acceptable. The longer, more arduous and more wearisome the work which they are given, the less they are paid; one can see workers who work strenuously and without interruption for sixteen hours a day, and who barely manage to earn the right not to die." [2]

[XV] " We are convinced . . . and the conviction is shared [in England] by the commissioners appointed to investigate the conditions of the handloom weavers, that the large towns would lose their working population in a short time if they did not constantly receive from the neighbouring countryside, a regular influx of healthy individuals, of new blood." [3]

---

[1] BURET, op. cit., p. 23. Emphasis added by Marx. [*Editor's note.*]
[2] Ibid., pp. 68–9. Quoted with minor omissions. [*Editor's note.*]
[3] Ibid., p. 362.

PROFIT OF CAPITAL

[1] (1) *Capital*

1. What is the basis of capital, i.e. of private ownership of the products of other men's labour? " . . . Even supposing that capital is not simply the fruit of robbery . . . it still needs the help of legislation in order to sanctify inheritance. . . . " [1]

How does one become an owner of productive stock? How does one become the possessor of the products which are created by means of this stock?

Through *positive law*.[2]

What does one acquire with capital, with the inheritance of a great property, for example?

" But the person who either acquires, or succeeds to a great fortune, does not necessarily acquire or succeed to any political power. . . . The power which that possession immediately and directly conveys to him, is the power of purchasing; a certain command over all the labour, or over all the produce of labour, which is then in the market." [3]

Capital is thus the *power of command* over labour and its products. The capitalist possesses this power, not on account of his personal or human qualities, but as the *owner* of capital. His power is the *purchasing* power of his capital, which nothing can withstand.

We shall see later how the capitalist, by means of capital, exercises his power of command over labour, and further, how capital itself rules the capitalist.

What is capital?

" It is, as it were, a certain quantity of labour stocked and stored up . . . " [4]

Capital is *stored-up labour*.

---

[1] JEAN-BAPTISTE SAY, *Traité d'économie politique*, 3ème édition, T. I–II. Paris, 1817. I, p. 136, footnote 2.

[2] Ibid., II, p. 4.   [3] SMITH, I, pp. 26–7.   [4] Ibid., p. 295.

2. *Fonds*, or stock, is any accumulation of products of the land or of manufacture. Stock is only called *capital* when it yields its owner a revenue or profit.[1]

(2) *The Profit of Capital*

The *profit or gain of capital* is altogether different from the *wages of labour*. The difference is manifested in two ways: first, the profits of capital are regulated altogether by the value of the stock employed; although the labour of inspection and direction may be the same for different amounts of capital. Furthermore, in large factories this whole labour is entrusted to some principal clerk, whose remuneration is not related to the [II] capital of which he oversees the management. Although the labour of the owner is in this case reduced almost to nothing, he still expects profits in proportion to his capital.[2]

Why does the capitalist demand this proportion between profit and capital?

He would have no *interest* in employing the workers unless he expected from the sale of their work something more than is necessary to replace the stock advanced by him as wages; and he would have no *interest* in employing a large stock rather than a small one if his profit were not in proportion to the extent of his stock.[3]

The capitalist makes a profit, therefore, first on the wages and secondly on the raw materials which he advances.

What relation, then, does profit have to capital?

If it is difficult to determine the average wages of labour at a particular time and place, it is all the more difficult to determine the profit on capital. Variations in the price of commodities which the capitalist deals in, the good or bad fortune of his rivals and customers, a thousand other accidents to which his goods are liable in transit and in warehouses, all produce a daily, almost hourly, fluctuation in profits.[4] But though it may be impossible to determine,

[1] SMITH, I, p. 243.   [2] Ibid., p. 43.   [3] Ibid., p. 42.   [4] Ibid., pp. 78–9.

with any precision, the average profits of capital, some notion may be formed of them from the *interest of money*. Wherever a great deal can be made by the use of money, a great deal will be given for the use of it; wherever little can be made, little will be given.[1] "The proportion which the usual market rate of interest ought to bear to the ordinary rate of clear profit, necessarily varies as profit rises or falls. Double interest is in Great Britain reckoned what the merchants call a good, moderate, reasonable profit, terms which . . . mean no more than a common and usual profit."[2]

The *lowest* rate of ordinary profit on capitals must always be *something more* than what is necessary to compensate the occasional losses to which every employment of capital is exposed. It is this surplus only which is the net or clear profit. The same holds for the lowest rate of interest.[3]

[III] The *highest rate* to which ordinary profits can rise is that which, in the price of the greater part of commodities, *eats up the whole of the rent of land* and reduces the wages of labour in the production and delivery of the commodity to the *lowest rate*, the bare subsistence of the labourer. The worker must always be fed in some way or other while he is engaged on the work; but the rent of land can disappear entirely. Example: the servants of the East India Company in Bengal.[4]

Besides all the advantages of limited competition which the capitalist is able to exploit in such a case, he can maintain the market price above the natural price by quite respectable means.

First, by *secrets in trade*, where the market is at a great distance from those who supply it; that is, by concealing a change in price, an increase above the natural level. The effect of this concealment is that other capitalists do not employ their capital in this sphere.

Next, by *secrets in manufacture*, which enable the capitalist to produce at lower cost, and to sell his goods at the same

[1] SMITH, I, p. 79. [2] Ibid., p. 87. [3] Ibid., p. 86. [4] Ibid., pp. 86-7.

price, or even at a lower price than his competitors, while making a higher profit. (Deceit by concealment is not immoral? Stock exchange dealings.) Furthermore, where production is confined to a particular locality (as in the case of choice wines) and the *effective demand* can never be satisfied. Finally, through monopolies granted to individuals or companies. Monopoly price is the highest that can be got.[1]

There are other fortuitous causes which can raise the profit on capital. The acquisition of new territory, or of new branches of trade, may sometimes raise the profit of stock even in a wealthy country, because part of the capital is withdrawn from the old branches of trade, competition is diminished, and the market is supplied with fewer goods, the prices of which then rise: those who deal in these goods can then afford to borrow at a higher rate of interest.[2]

As any commodity comes to be more manufactured, that part of the price which resolves itself into wages and profit comes to be greater in proportion to that which resolves itself into rent. In the progress of the manufacture of a commodity, not only do the number of the profits increase, but every subsequent profit is greater than the preceding one, because the capital from which [IV] it is derived must always be greater. The capital which employs the weavers, for example, must be greater than that which employs the spinners; because it not only replaces that capital with its profits, but pays, besides, the wages of the weavers; and the profits must always bear some proportion to the capital.[3]

Thus the increasing part which human labour, compared with raw material, plays in the manufactured product does not increase the wages of labour but increases partly the number of capitals and partly the size of every subsequent capital in relation to that which precedes it.

More will be said later about the profit which the capitalist derives from the division of labour.

He profits doubly, first from the division of labour, and

---

[1] SMITH, I, pp. 53-4.   [2] Ibid., p. 83.   [3] Ibid., p. 45.

secondly, above all, from the increasing share of human labour, as against raw material. The greater the human contribution to a commodity, the greater is the profit of dead capital.

In the same society the average rates of profit on capital are more nearly upon a level than are the wages of different kinds of labour.[1] In the different employments of capital, the ordinary rate of profit varies with the certainty or uncertainty of the return. " . . . the ordinary profit of stock, though it rises with the risk, does not always seem to rise in proportion to it." [2]

It goes without saying that the profits of capital also rise if the means of circulation become less expensive or more easily available (e.g. paper money).

(3) *The Rule of Capital over Labour and the Motives of the Capitalist*

" The consideration of his own private profit is the sole motive which determines the owner of any capital to employ it either in agriculture, in manufactures, or in some particular branch of the wholesale or retail trade. The different quantities of productive labour which it may put into motion, and the different values which it may add to the annual produce of the land and labour of the society, according as it is employed in one or other of those different ways, never enter into his thoughts." [3]

" The most useful employment of capital for the capitalist is that which, with the same degree of security, yields him the largest profit; but this employment is not always the most useful for society, . . . the most useful [for a nation] is that which . . . stimulates the productive power of its land and labour." [4]

" The plans and projects of the employers of stock regulate and direct all the most important operations of labour, and

---

[1] SMITH, I, p. 45.   [2] Ibid., pp. 99–100.   [3] Ibid., p. 335.
[4] SAY, op. cit., II., pp. 130–1.   Marx paraphrases this passage.   [*Editor's note.*]

profit is the end proposed by all those plans and projects. But the rate of profit does not, like rent and wages, rise with the prosperity and fall with the declension of the society. On the contrary, it is naturally low in rich and high in poor countries, and it is always highest in the countries which are going fastest to ruin. The interest of this third order, [those who live by profit. *Editor*] therefore, has not the same connexion with the general interest of the society as that of the other two. . . . The interest of the dealers, however, in any particular branch of trade or manufactures, is always in some respects different from, and even opposite to, that of the public. To widen the market and to narrow the competition, is always the interest of the dealers . . . an order of men whose interest is never exactly the same with that of the public, who have generally an interest to deceive and even to oppress the public. . . . " [1]

(4) *The Accumulation of Capitals and the Competition among Capitalists*

The *increase of capitals*, which raises wages, tends to lower profits, because of the *competition* among capitalists.[2]

If, for example, the capital which is necessary for the grocery trade of a particular town " is divided between two different grocers, their competition will tend to make both of them sell cheaper than if it were in the hands of one only; and if it were divided among twenty, their competition would be just so much the greater, and the chance of their combining together, in order to raise the price, just so much the less." [3]

Since we already know that monopoly prices are as high as possible, since the interest of the capitalists, even from the ordinary viewpoint of political economy, is in opposition to the interest of society, and since an increase in profits has an effect upon prices like that of compound interest, it follows that the only protection against the capitalists is *competition*,

[1] SMITH, op. cit., I, pp. 231-2.　　　[2] Ibid., p. 78.　　　[3] Ibid., p. 322.

which according to the evidence of political economy has the salutary effect of raising wages and reducing the prices of goods, to the advantage of the consuming public.

But competition is only possible if capitals multiply and are held in many hands. The formation of many capitals is only possible as a result of widespread accumulation, but widespread accumulation inevitably turns into accumulation by a few. Competition between capitals increases the concentration of capitals. Accumulation, which means, under the rule of private property, *concentration* of capital in a few hands, is a necessary consequence when capitals are left free to follow their natural course. It is through competition that the way is made clear for this natural tendency of capital.

We have seen that the profit of capital is proportionate to its size. Thus a large capital accumulates more rapidly, in proportion to its size, than does a small capital, quite apart from any deliberate competition.

[VIII] Accordingly the accumulation of large capital is much more rapid than that of smaller capital, even disregarding competition. But let us follow this process further.

With the increase of capitals, the profits of capitals diminish, as a result of competition. Thus the first to suffer is the small capitalist.

Further, the increase of capitals, and the existence of a large number of capitalists, presupposes a condition of increasing wealth in a country.

" In a country which had acquired its full complement of riches, . . . as the ordinary rate of clear profit would be very small, so the usual market rate of interest which could be afforded out of it would be so low as to render it impossible for any but the very wealthiest people to live upon the interest of their money. All people of small or middling fortunes would be obliged to superintend themselves the employment of their own stocks. It would be necessary that almost every man should be a man of business, or engage in some sort of trade." [1]

This is the situation most dear to the heart of political economy.

" The proportion between capital and revenue, therefore, seems everywhere to regulate the proportion between industry and idleness. Wherever capital predominates, industry prevails: wherever revenue, idleness." [2]

What about the employment of capital in this situation of increased competition?

" As the quantity of stock to be lent at interest increases, the interest, or the price which must be paid for the use of that stock, necessarily diminishes, not only from those general causes, which make the market price of things commonly diminish as their quantity increases, but from other causes which are peculiar to this particular case. As capitals increase in any country, the profits which can be made by employing them necessarily diminish. It becomes gradually more and more difficult to find within the country a profitable method of employing any new capital. There arises in consequence a competition between different capitals, the owner of one endeavouring to get possession of that employment which is occupied by another. But upon most occasions he can hope to jostle that other out of this employment by no other means but by dealing upon more reasonable terms. He must not only sell what he deals in somewhat cheaper, but in order to get it to sell, he must sometimes, too, buy it dearer. The demand for productive labour, by the increase of the funds which are destined for maintaining it, grows every day greater and greater. Labourers easily find employment, [IX] but the owners of capitals find it difficult to get labourers to employ. Their competition raises the wages of labour and sinks the profits of stock." [3]

Thus the small capitalist has the choice, either (1) to

<hr />

[1] Smith, I, p. 86.   [2] Ibid., p. 301.   [3] Ibid., p. 316.

consume his capital since he can no longer live upon the interest, and thus cease to be a capitalist, or (2) to set up in business himself, sell his goods cheaper and buy dearer than the wealthier capitalist, and pay higher wages, and thus ruin himself, since the market price is already low as a result of the intense competition which we have presupposed. If, on the other hand, the large capitalist wants to squeeze out the smaller capitalist, he has the same advantage over him as the capitalist has over the worker. The larger amount of his capital compensates him for the smaller profits, and he can support short-term losses until the smaller capitalist is ruined and he finds himself free of this competition. Thus he accumulates the profits of the small capitalist.

Furthermore: the large capitalist always buys more cheaply than the small capitalist, because he buys in larger quantities. Consequently, he can afford to sell more cheaply.

But if the fall in the rate of interest turns the medium capitalists from rentiers into businessmen, the increase in business capitals and the resulting lower rate of profit bring about, in turn, a fall in the rate of interest.

" But when the profits which can be made by the use of a capital are . . . diminished . . . the price which can be paid for the use of it, . . . must necessarily be diminished with them." [1]

" As riches, improvement, and population have increased, interest has declined," and consequently the profits of stock " . . . after these are diminished, stock may not only continue to increase, but to increase much faster than before. . . . A great stock, though with small profits, generally increases faster than a small stock with great profits. Money, says the proverb, makes money." [2]

If, therefore, this large capital is opposed by small capitals with small profits, as happens under the assumed conditions of intense competition, it completely crushes them. The inevitable consequence of this competition is a general

[1] SMITH, I, p. 316.   [2] Ibid., p. 83.

deterioration of goods, adulteration, shoddy production, universal contamination, as is found in large towns.

[X] Another important feature in the competition between large and small capitals is the relationship between *fixed capital* and *circulating capital*.

Circulating capital is capital " employed in raising, manufacturing or purchasing goods, and selling them again with a profit. The capital employed in this manner yields no revenue or profit to its employer, while it either remains in his possession or continues in the same shape. . . . His capital is continually going from him in one shape, and returning to him in another, and it is only by means of such circulation, or successive exchanges, that it can yield him any profit . . . " *Fixed capital* is capital " employed in the improvement of land, in the purchase of useful machines and instruments, or in such like things . . . "

" . . . every saving in the expense of supporting the fixed capital is an improvement of the net revenue [of the society]. The whole capital of the undertaker of every work is necessarily divided between his fixed and his circulating capital. While his whole capital remains the same, the smaller the one part, the greater must necessarily be the other. It is the circulating capital which furnishes the materials and wages of labour, and puts industry into motion. Every saving therefore, in the expense of maintaining the fixed capital, which does not diminish the productive powers of labour, must increase the fund which puts industry into motion, . . . " [1]

It will be seen at once that the relation between fixed and circulating capital is much more favourable in the case of the large capitalist than in that of the smaller capitalist. The additional fixed capital required by a great banker, compared with a very small one, is insignificant. Their fixed capital is limited to an office. The equipment of a large landowner does not increase in proportion to the size of his

[1] Smith, I, p. 257.

estate. Similarly, the credit which a large capitalist enjoys, in comparison with a smaller one, also represents a greater saving in fixed capital, namely in the amount of ready money which he must have available. It is clear, finally, that where industrial labour has reached an advanced stage in which almost all manual labour has become factory labour, the entire capital of a small capitalist does not suffice to provide him even with the necessary fixed capital. It is well known that large scale cultivation ordinarily provides employment only for a small number of hands.

In general a concentration and rationalization of fixed capital occurs with the accumulation of large amounts of capital, in comparison with the small capitalists. The large capitalist introduces for himself some kind of organization of the instruments of labour.

" Similarly, in the sphere of industry, every factory is a comprehensive co-ordination of extensive material property with numerous and diversified intellectual abilities and technical skills, for the *common* purpose of production. . . . Where legislation maintains large landed property, the surplus of a growing population crowds into the workshops; and it is, therefore, the field of industry where the greater part of the proletarians are massed, as in Great Britain. But where legislation allows the continuous partition of land, as in France, the number of small, debt-ridden proprietors increases, and they are thrust into the class of the needy and unsatisfied by the continuous subdivision of land. If, finally, this subdivision and indebtedness reaches a high level, then the small proprietors are absorbed again by the great landowners, just as small industry is destroyed by large-scale industry. Since, in this case, large landholdings are reconstituted, the propertyless workers who are no longer needed for the cultivation of the land are again driven into industry." [1]

" The nature of commodities of the same kind is changed

---

[1] SCHULZ, op. cit., pp. 58–9.

by the changes in the mode of production, and notably by the use of machinery. Simply by eliminating human labour, it has become possible to spin from a pound of cotton worth 3s. 8d., 350 hanks amounting to 167 English (or 36 German) miles in length, of a value of 25 guineas." [1]

" On average the prices of cotton goods in England have fallen by eleven-twelfths in the past forty-five years. According to Marshall's calculations the same quantity of products which cost sixteen shillings in 1814 can now be supplied for 1s. 10d. The greater cheapness of industrial products has increased internal consumption and the external market, and with this is connected the fact that in Britain the number of workers in the cotton industry has not only not diminished since the introduction of machinery, but has increased from forty thousand to one and a half million. [XII] As regards the earnings of industrial entrepreneurs and workers, the growing competition among factory owners has necessarily reduced their profits in relation to the quantity of products. Between 1820 and 1833 the gross profit of Manchester producers on a piece of calico fell from 4s. 1⅓d. to 1s. 9d. But in order to compensate this loss the scale of production has been greatly extended. The result is . . . that in some branches of the industry partial overproduction occurs; that there are frequent bankruptcies, which produce fluctuations of property *within* the class of the capitalists and lords of labour, and cast a proportion of those who are economically ruined into the proletariat; and that there are frequent and sudden increases or decreases in the demand for labour, the hardships of which are always bitterly experienced by the class of wage earners." [2]

" To hire out one's labour is to begin one's enslavement; to hire out the material of labour is to establish one's liberty. . . . Labour is man, but material contains nothing of man." [3]

[1] SCHULZ, op. cit., p. 62.   [2] Ibid., p. 63.
[3] PECQUEUR, op. cit., pp. 411-12.

" The *material* element which can do nothing to create wealth without the element of *labour*, receives the magical power of being fruitful for them [property owners] as if they themselves had contributed this indispensable element." [1] " If we assume that the daily labour of a worker brings him an average of 400 francs a year, and that this sum is enough for an adult to live at subsistence level, then every property owner who receives 2,000 francs in interest, tithes, rent, etc. indirectly obliges five men to work for him; 100,000 francs in interest represents the labour of 250 men, and 1,000,000 francs the labour of 2,500 individuals.[2] Consequently, 300 million (Louis Philippe) represents the labour of 750,000 workers.

" The owners of property have obtained from human legislation the right to use and to abuse, i.e. to do as they please with the materials of all labour . . . they are not in the least obliged by law to provide work for the non-owners as it is needed, or invariably; nor are they obliged to pay a wage which is always adequate, etc." [3]

" Complete freedom as regards the nature, quantity, quality, and occasion of production, and as regards the use and consumption of wealth, the disposal of the materials of labour. Everyone is free to exchange what he possesses as he chooses, without regard to anything but his own self-interest."

" Competition simply expresses voluntary exchange, which itself is the logical consequence of the individual right to use and abuse the instruments of production. These three economic factors, which form a unity—the right to use and abuse, free exchange, and arbitrary competition—have the following consequences: everyone produces what he will, how, when and where he will, produces well or ill, too much or not enough, too soon or too late, too dear or too cheap. No one knows whether he will be able to sell his product, or how, when, where or to whom he will sell it;

---

[1] PECQUEUR, op. cit., p. 412.   [2] Ibid., pp. 412–13.   [3] Ibid., p. 413.

and the same applies to purchases. The producer does not know what are the needs and resources, the demand and supply. He sells when he likes or when he can, where he likes, to whom he likes and at the price he chooses. He buys in the same manner. In all this he is the plaything of chance, the slave of the law of the strongest, of the least pressed for time, of the richest . . . While there is great need at one point, there is surfeit and waste at another. While one producer sells much, or sells at high prices, and makes enormous profits, another sells nothing or sells at a loss . . . Supply knows nothing of the demand, and demand knows nothing of the supply. You produce on the strength of a taste or fashion which appears in the consuming public, but when you are ready to supply the goods, taste has already changed and has become attached to some other kind of product . . . the inevitable consequences, continual and widespread bankruptcies, frauds, sudden ruin and unexpected fortunes, commercial crises, unemployment, periodical surpluses or shortages, instability and swallowing up of wages and profits, massive lossses or waste of wealth, time and effort in the arena of desperate competition." [1]

Ricardo, in his book (rent of land): [2] The nations are only workshops. Man is a machine for consuming and producing, human life a capital. Economic laws rule the world blindly. For Ricardo men are nothing, the product is everything.[3] In Chapter 26 of the French translation [4] we read: " To an individual with a capital of £20,000, whose profits were £2,000 per annum, it would be a matter quite indifferent whether his capital would employ a

---

[1] PECQUEUR, op. cit., pp. 414–16.

[2] DAVID RICARDO, *Principles of Political Economy and Taxation*, London, 1816, Chapter II, " On Rent."

[3] These statements are not quoted from Ricardo but are Marx's own elaborations of J. B. Say's critical comments in Chapter 26 of the French edition of the book. *See* the following note. [*Editor's note.*]

[4] *Des principes de l'économie politique et de l'impôt* par David Ricardo, traduit de l'anglais par F. S. Constancio avec des notes explicatives et critiques par J. B. Say. 2ème édition. T. I–II. Paris, 1835, Ch. XXVI, " Du revenu brut et du revenu net."

hundred or a thousand men . . . is not the real interest of the nation similar? Provided its net real income, its rents and profits, be the same, it is of no importance whether the nation consists of ten or of twelve millions of inhabitants." [1]
" In truth," says M. de Sismondi, " it remains only to desire that the king, left alone in the island, should, by turning a handle, get all the work of England performed by automatons." [2]

" . . . the master who buys the labour of the worker at a price so low that it barely suffices to meet the most urgent needs, is responsible neither for the inadequacy of wages nor for the excessive hours of work; he is also subject to the law which he imposes. . . . it is not so much from men as from the power of things that misery comes." [3]

" The inhabitants of many different parts of Great Britain have not capital sufficient to improve and cultivate all their lands. The wool of the southern counties of Scotland is, a great part of it, after a long land carriage through very bad roads, manufactured in Yorkshire, for want of capital to manufacture it at home. There are many little manufacturing towns in Great Britain, of which the inhabitants have not capital sufficient to transport the produce of their own industry to those distant markets where there is demand and consumption for it. If there are any merchants among them, [XIV] they are properly only the agents of wealthier merchants who reside in some of the greater commercial cities." [4] " The annual produce of the land and labour of any nation can be increased in its value by no other means but by increasing either the number of its productive labourers, or the productive powers of those labourers who

---

[1] RICARDO, op. cit. (Everyman edition), pp. 234–5. Marx quotes from the French edition: *see* the previous note. [*Editor's note.*]
[2] J. C. L. SIMONDE DE SISMONDI, *Nouveaux principes d'économie politique.* T. I–II. Paris, 1819. II, p. 331.
[3] BURET, op. cit., I, p. 82.
[4] SMITH, op. cit., I, pp. 326–7.

had before been employed." In either case, an increase of capital is almost always necessary.[1]

" As the accumulation of stock must, in the nature of things, be previous to the division of labour, so labour can be more and more subdivided in proportion only as stock is previously more and more accumulated. The quantity of materials which the same number of people can work up, increases in a great proportion as labour comes to be more and more subdivided; and as the operations of each workman are gradually reduced to a greater degree of simplicity, a variety of new machines come to be invented for facilitating and abridging these operations. As the division of labour advances, therefore, in order to give constant employment to an equal number of workmen, an equal stock of provisions, and a greater stock of materials and tools than what would have been necessary in a ruder state of things, must be accumulated beforehand. But the number of workmen in every branch of business generally increases with the division of labour in that branch, or rather it is the increase of their number which enables them to class and subdivide themselves in this manner." [2]

" As the accumulation of stock is previously necessary for carrying on this great improvement in the productive powers of labour, so that accumulation naturally leads to this improvement. The person who employs his stock in maintaining labour, necessarily wishes to employ it in such a manner as to produce as great a quantity of work as possible. He endeavours, therefore, both to make among his workmen the most proper distribution of employment, and to furnish them with the best machines which he can either invent or afford to purchase. His abilities in both these respects are generally in proportion to the extent of his stock, or to the number of people it can employ. The quantity of industry, therefore, not only increases in every country

[1] SMITH, op. cit., I, pp. 306–7.
[2] Ibid., pp. 241–2.

with the increase of the stock which employs it, but, in consequence of that increase, the same quantity of industry produces a much greater quantity of work." [1] Hence *over-production*.

" Wider combinations of productive forces . . . in industry and trade through the combination of more numerous and diverse human and natural powers for enterprise on a larger scale. Already here and there, closer interrelations among the principal branches of production. Thus large manufacturers will seek to acquire large estates, in order to be able to obtain directly at least a part of the necessary raw material of their industry; or they will establish a trading organization in connexion with their industry, not only for the sale of their own products, but also for the purchase of other commodities and their resale to their workers. In England, a number of factory owners control 10,000–12,000 workers . . . , and such combinations of several branches of production under *one* directing mind, such small states or provinces within a state, are already not uncommon. Thus, the mine-owners near *Birmingham* recently took over the *whole* process of iron-smelting which was previously divided among several entrepreneurs and owners.[2] Finally, we see in the large joint-stock companies which have become so numerous, extensive combinations of the money resources of *many* shareholders with the scientific and technical knowledge of others who take on the management of the work. Thereby, it is possible for the capitalists to utilize their savings in many branches of production, and indeed to spread them over agricultural, industrial and commercial production. Thus their interests also become many-sided, [XVI] and the conflicts of interest between agriculture, industry and trade are moderated and fused. But

---

[1] SMITH, op. cit., I, p. 242.

[2] This sentence is from a footnote in the original which refers to *Deutsche Vierteljahresschrift*, Stuttgart und Tübingen, 1838 (Erster Jahrgang) Heft 3, p. 47 *et seq.* " Der bergmännische Distrikt zwischen Birmingham und Wolverhampton." Von A. von Treskow.

these greater opportunities to employ capital fruitfully in the most varied ways must increase the conflict between the owning and non-owning classes." [1]

The monstrous profit which the landlord of dwelling houses gains from the poor. The greater the industrial misery, the higher is the rent.

Similarly with the interest obtained from the vices of the ruined proletarians. (Prostitution, drunkenness, the pawn-broker.) The accumulation of capitals increases, and the competition between them diminishes, when capital and landed property are united in the same hands and when capital is enabled by its size to combine different branches of production.

Indifference towards men. Smith's [2] twenty lottery tickets. [3]

Say's net and gross revenue.

[1] Schulz, op. cit., pp. 40–1.

[2] This appears as *Swift's* in the *MEGA* edition. [*Editor's note.*]

[3] Smith, op. cit., I, p. 94. "In a perfectly fair lottery, those who draw the prizes ought to gain all that is lost by those who draw the blanks. In a profession where twenty fail for one that succeeds, that one ought to gain all that should have been gained by the unsuccessful twenty." [*Editor's note.*]

RENT OF LAND

[I] THE *right of landownership* has its source in robbery.[1] Landlords, like all other men, love to reap where they never sowed, and demand a rent even for the natural produce of the land.[2]

" The rent of land, it may be thought, is frequently no more than a reasonable profit or interest for the stock laid out by the landlord upon its improvement. This, no doubt, may be partly the case upon some occasions. . . . The landlord demands a rent even for unimproved land, and the supposed interest or profit upon the expense of improvement is generally an addition to this original rent. Those improvements, besides, are not always made by the stock of the landlord, but sometimes by that of the tenant. When the lease comes to be renewed, however, the landlord commonly demands the same augmentation of rent as if they had been all made by his own.

" He sometimes demands rent for what is altogether incapable of human improvement." [3]

Smith gives as an example of this latter case, kelp, a species of seaweed, which when burnt, yields an alkaline salt, useful for making glass, soap, etc. It grows in several parts of Great Britain, especially in Scotland, but only upon rocks which lie within the high water mark, which are covered by the sea twice a day, and of which the produce, therefore, was never augmented by human industry. The landlord of such a kelp shore, however, demands a rent for it just as much as for his corn fields. In the neighbourhood of the Islands of Shetland the sea is uncommonly abundant in fish. A large part of their inhabitants [II] live by fishing. But in

---

[1] SAY, op. cit., I, p. 136, footnote 2.
[2] SMITH, op. cit., I, p. 44.
[3] Ibid., p. 131.

order to profit by the produce of the sea they must have a habitation upon the neighbouring land. The rent of the landlord is in proportion, not to what the farmer can make by the land, but to what he can make both by the land and by the sea.[1]

" This rent may be considered as the produce of those powers of nature, the use of which the landlord lends to the farmer. It is greater or smaller according to the supposed extent of those powers, or in other words, according to the supposed natural or improved fertility of the land. It is the work of nature which remains after deducting or compensating everything which can be regarded as the work of man." [2]

" The rent of land, therefore, considered as the price paid for the use of land, is naturally a monopoly price. It is not at all proportioned to what the landlord may have laid out upon the improvement of the land, or to what he can afford to take; but to what the farmer can afford to give." [3]

" They [the proprietors of land] are the only one of the three orders whose revenue costs them neither labour nor care, but comes to them, as it were, of its own accord, and independent of any plan or project of their own." [4]

We have already learnt that the amount of rent depends upon the degree of *fertility* of the land.

Another factor in its determination is *situation*.

" The rent of land not only varies with its fertility, whatever be its produce, but with its situation, whatever be its fertility." [5]

" The produce of land, mines and fisheries, when their natural fertility is equal, is in proportion to the extent [III] and proper application of the capitals employed about them. When the capitals are equal and equally well applied, it is in proportion to their natural fertility." [6]

[1] SMITH, op. cit., I, p. 131.
[2] Ibid., pp. 324–5.
[3] Ibid., p. 131.
[4] Ibid., p. 230.
[5] Ibid., p. 133.
[6] Ibid., p. 249.

These propositions of Smith are important, because they relate the rent of land, given equal costs of production and capital of equal size, to the greater or lesser fertility of the soil. Thus they show clearly the perversion of concepts in political economy, which transforms the fertility of the soil into an attribute of the landowner.

But let us now examine the rent of land as it is determined in real life.

The rent of land is established by the *struggle between tenant and landlord*. In all political economy we find that the hostile opposition of interests, struggle and warfare, are recognized as the basis of social organization.

Let us now see what are the relations between landlord and tenant.

" In adjusting the terms of the lease, the landlord endeavours to leave him no greater share of the produce than what is sufficient to keep up the stock from which he furnishes the seed, pays the labour, and purchases and maintains the cattle and other instruments of husbandry, together with the ordinary profits of farming stock in the neighbourhood. This is evidently the smallest share with which the tenant can content himself without being a loser, and the landlord seldom means to leave him any more. Whatever part of the produce, or, what is the same thing, whatever part of its price is over and above this share, he naturally endeavours to reserve himself as the rent of his land, which is evidently the highest the tenant can afford to pay in the actual circumstances of the land. [IV] . . . This portion . . . may still be considered as the natural rent of land, or the rent for which it is naturally meant that land should for the most part be let." [1]

" The landlords," observes Say, " operate a particular kind of monopoly against the tenants. The demand for their commodity, the land, can go on expanding indefinitely; but there is only a limited amount of their commodity . . .

---

[1] SMITH, op. cit., I, pp. 130–1.

The bargain struck between landlord and tenant is always as advantageous as possible to the former . . . Besides the advantage which the landlord derives from the nature of the case, he derives a further advantage from his position, which gives him a larger fortune and sometimes a greater credit and standing. But the first by itself is enough to ensure that he will always be able to profit from the favourable situation of the land. The opening of a canal, or a road; the increase of population and of the prosperity of a district, always raise the rent . . . Indeed the tenant himself may improve the land at his own expense, but he only enjoys the profit from this capital for the duration of his lease, on the expiry of which, since the capital cannot be removed, it remains with the landowner. Thereafter it is the latter who reaps the interest without having made the outlay, for there is now a proportionate increase in the rent." [1]

" Rent, considered as the price paid for the use of land, is naturally the highest which the tenant can afford to pay in the actual circumstances of the land." [2]

" The rent of an estate above ground commonly amounts to what is supposed to be a third of the gross produce; and it is generally a rent certain and independent of the occasional variations [V] in the crop." [3]   Rent " is seldom less than a fourth, and frequently more than a third of the whole produce." [4]

Rent cannot be paid in the case of all commodities. For example, in many districts no rent is paid for building stone.

" Such parts only of the produce of land can commonly be brought to market of which the ordinary price is sufficient to replace the stock which must be employed in bringing them thither, together with its ordinary profits. If the ordinary price is more than this, the surplus part of it will naturally go to the rent of the land. If it is not more, though the

[1] SAY, op. cit., II, pp. 142–3. Marx quotes this passage with minor variations. [*Editor's note.*]

[2] SMITH, op. cit., I, p. 130.   [3] Ibid., p. 153.   [4] Ibid., p. 325.

commodity may be brought to market, it can afford no rent to the landlord. Whether the price is or is not more depends upon the demand." [1]

" Rent, it is to be observed, therefore, enters into the composition of the price of commodities in a different way from wages and profit. High or low wages and profit are the causes of high or low price; high or low rent is the effect of it." [2]

Among the *products* which always afford a *rent* is *food*.

" As men, like all other animals, naturally multiply in proportion to the means of their subsistence, food is always, more or less, in demand. It can always purchase or command a greater or smaller quantity of labour, and somebody can always be found who is willing to do something in order to obtain it. The quantity of labour, indeed, which it can purchase is not always equal to what it could maintain, if managed in the most economical manner, on account of the high wages which are sometimes given to labour. But it can always purchase such a quantity of labour as it can maintain, according to the rate at which that sort of labour is commonly maintained in the neighbourhood.

" But land, in almost any situation, produces a greater quantity of food than what is sufficient to maintain all the labour necessary for bringing it to market in the most liberal way in which that labour is ever maintained. The surplus, too, is always more than sufficient to replace the stock which employed that labour, together with its profits. Something, therefore, always remains for a rent to the landlord." [3]

" Food is in this manner not only the original source of rent, but every other part of the produce of land which afterwards affords rent derives that part of its value from the improvement of the powers of labour in producing food by means of the improvement and cultivation of land." [4]

" Human food seems to be the only produce of land which

[1] SMITH, op. cit., I, p. 132.   [2] Ibid., p. 132.
[3] Ibid., pp. 132–3.   [4] Ibid., p. 150.

always and necessarily affords a rent to the landlord." [1]
" Countries are populous not in proportion to the number of
people whom their produce can clothe and lodge, but in
proportion to that of those whom it can feed." [2]

" After food, clothing and lodging are the two great wants
of mankind." [3] They usually afford a rent, but not necessarily and invariably.

[VIII] Let us now see how the landlord exploits everything which benefits society.

1. The rent of land increases with increasing population.[4]

2. We have already learnt from Say how the rent of
land increases with the building of railways, etc., and with
the improvement, security and multiplication of the means
of communication.

3. " . . . every improvement in the circumstances of
the society tends either directly or indirectly to raise the
real rent of land, to increase the real wealth of the landlord, his power of purchasing the labour, or the produce
of the labour of other people."

" The extension of improvement and cultivation tends
to raise it directly. The landlord's share of the produce
necessarily increases with the increase of the produce."

" That rise in the real price of those parts of the rude
produce of land, . . . the rise in the price of cattle, for
example, tends too to raise the rent of land directly, and
in a still greater proportion. The real value of the landlord's share, his real command of the labour of other
people, not only rises with the real value of the produce,
but the proportion of his share to the whole produce rises
with it. That produce, after the rise in its real price,
requires no more labour to collect it than before. A
smaller proportion of it will, therefore, be sufficient to
replace, with the ordinary profit, the stock which employs

---

[1] SMITH, op. cit., I, p. 147.   [2] Ibid., p. 149.
[3] Ibid., p. 147.   [4] Ibid., p. 146.

that labour. A greater proportion of it must, consequently, belong to the landlord." [1]

The greater demand for raw products, and, therefore, the rise in their value, may result in part from the increase of population and from the increase in their needs. But every new invention, every new application in manufacture of a hitherto unused or little-used raw material increases the rent of the land. Thus, for example, there was a tremendous rise in the rent of coal-mines with the advent of the railways, steamships, etc.

Besides this advantage which the landlord derives from manufacture, discoveries and labour, there is another which we shall see presently.

4. " All those improvements in the productive powers of labour, which tend directly to reduce the real price of manufactures, tend indirectly to raise the real rent of land. The landlord exchanges that part of his rude produce, which is over and above his own consumption, or what comes to the same thing, the price of that part of it, for manufactured produce. Whatever reduces the real price of the latter, raises that of the former. An equal quantity of the former becomes thereby equivalent to a greater quantity of the latter; and the landlord is enabled to purchase a greater quantity of the conveniencies, ornaments or luxuries, which he has occasion for." [2]

It is absurd to conclude, however, as Smith does, that since the landlord exploits everything which benefits society, [X] the interest of the landlord is always identical with that of society.[3] In the economic system under the domination of private property, the interest which an individual has in society is in exactly inverse proportion to the interest which society has in him—just as the interest of the moneylender in the spendthrift is by no means identical with the interest of the spendthrift.

[1] Smith, op. cit., I, pp. 228–9.   [2] Ibid., p. 229.   [3] Ibid., p. 230.

We mention only in passing the landlord's obsession with monopoly directed against the landed property of foreign countries, from which the corn laws, for instance, derive. Equally, we pass over here, medieval serfdom, slavery in the colonies, and the miserable conditions of the rural population, the day-labourers, in Great Britain. Let us confine ourselves to the propositions of political economy itself.

1. The interest of the landlord in the well-being of society means, according to the principles of political economy, that he is interested in the growth of population and production, and the increase of needs, in short in the increase of wealth; and the increase of wealth is, according to our previous observations, identical with the increase of misery and enslavement. The developing relationship between rent and misery is an example of the landowner's interest in society, for with the increase in rent the ground rent (the interest on the land on which the house stands) also rises.

2. According to the economists themselves the interest of the landowner is bitterly opposed to the interest of the tenant, and hence to a large section of society.

[XI] 3. Since the landowner can demand more rent from the tenant the less the latter pays in wages, and since the tenant reduces wages more the more rent the landowner demands, the interest of the landowner is just as bitterly opposed to the interest of the agricultural labourers as is the interest of the manufacturer to that of his workers. It forces wages down to a minimum.

4. Since a real reduction in the price of manufactured goods increases the rent of land, the landowner has a direct interest in depressing the wages oᶠ industrial workers, in the growth of competition between capitalists, in overproduction, in industrial misery.

5. Thus, the interest of the landowner, far from being identical with that of society, is bitterly opposed to the

interests of the tenants, the agricultural labourers, the industrial workers and the capitalists; and the interest of one landowner is not even identical with that of another, on account of competition, which we have now to consider.

In general, large landed property and small landed property stand in the same relation to each other as do large capital and small capital. There are, however, special circumstances which bring about directly the accumulation of large landed property and thereby the circumscription of small property.

[XII] 1. Nowhere does the number of workers and implements diminish so greatly in relation to the size of the funds employed as in the case of landed property. And nowhere does the possibility of many-sided exploitation, the saving of costs of production and the rational division of labour, increase proportionately more with the size of the funds employed. A plot of land may be as small as you like, but the implements required, plough, saw, etc., have a limit below which they cannot be reduced, while there is no limit to the reduction in the size of the plot.

2. Large landed property accumulates the interest which the tenant's capital has produced by improving the land and the soil. Small landed property has to use its own capital; and this particular profit disappears.

3. Whereas every improvement in society benefits the large estate, it harms the small estate since it makes necessary a larger supply of ready cash.

4. There are two further laws of this competition to consider—

(a) " . . . the rent of the cultivated land, of which the produce is human food, regulates the rent of the greater part of the other cultivated land." [1]

[1] Smith, op. cit., I, p. 144.

In the last resort only the large estate can produce food such as cattle, etc.; it can, therefore, determine the rent of other land and reduce it to a minimum.

The small landowner who works on his own account stands, therefore, in the same relation to the large landowner as does the artisan who possesses his *own* tools to the factory owner. The small estate has become merely a tool. [XVI] For the small landowner rent of land disappears entirely, and there remains at most the interest on his capital and the wages of his labour, since rent can be depressed to such an extent by competition that it becomes no more than the interest on capital which is not invested by the owner himself.

(β) Furthermore, we have already seen that given equal fertility and equally efficient exploitation of lands, mines and fisheries, the produce is proportionate to the amount of capital employed. Thus, the victory of the large landowner. Similarly, where equal amounts of capital are employed the produce is proportionate to fertility. Where capitals are equal the owner of the more fertile land triumphs.

(γ) " The most fertile coal-mine, too, regulates the price of coals at all the other mines in its neighbourhood. Both the proprietor and the undertaker of the work find, the one that he can get a greater rent, the other that he can get a greater profit by somewhat underselling all their neighbours. Their neighbours are soon obliged to sell at the same price, though they cannot so well afford it, and though it always diminishes, and sometimes takes away altogether both their rent and their profit. Some works are abandoned altogether; others can afford no rent, and can be wrought only by the proprietor." [1] " After the discovery of the mines of Peru, the silver mines of Europe were, the greater part of them, abandoned . . . This was the case, too,

[1] SMITH, op. cit., I, pp. 152–3.

with the ancient mines of Peru, after the discovery of those of Potosi." [1] What Smith says here about the mines is more or less valid for landed property in general.

(δ) " The ordinary market price of land, it is to be observed, depends everywhere upon the ordinary market rate of interest . . . if the rent of land should fall short of the interest of money by a greater difference, nobody would buy land, which would soon reduce its ordinary price. On the contrary, if the advantages should much more than compensate the difference, everybody would buy land, which would soon raise its ordinary price." [2] It follows from this relation between rent of land and interest on money that rent must continue to decrease until finally only the wealthiest people can live on rent. Hence the competition between landowners who do not lease their land to tenants increases. Some of the landowners are ruined and there is further accumulation of large landed property.

[XVII] This competition has the further consequence that a large part of landed property falls into the hands of capitalists, who then become landed proprietors; while the smaller landowners, generally speaking, are already nothing but capitalists. Thus a part of large landed property becomes industrial property.

The final result is, therefore, the abolition of the distinction between capitalist and landowner, so that broadly speaking there remain only two classes in the population, the working class and the capitalist class. This disposal of landed property and transformation of the land into a commodity is the final ruin of the old aristocracy and the complete triumph of the aristocracy of money.

1. Romanticism sheds many sentimental tears over this event, but we shall not do so. Romanticism always confuses

---

[1] SMITH, op. cit., I, p. 154.   [2] Ibid., p. 320.

the infamy involved in this *disposal of land* with the wholly reasonable and, within the system of private property, necessary and desirable consequences of the *disposal of landed property*. In the first place, feudal landed property is already essentially land which has been disposed of, alienated from men and now confronting them in the shape of a few great lords.

Already in feudal landownership the ownership of the soil appears as an alien power ruling over men. The serf is the product of the land. In the same way, the heir, the first-born son, belongs to the land. It inherits him. The rule of private property begins with the ownership of land, which is its basis. But in feudal landownership the lord *appears* at least as king of the land. Likewise, there is the appearance of a more intimate connexion between the owner and the land than is the case in the possession of mere *wealth*. Landed property assumes an individual character with its lord, has its own status, is knightly or baronial with him, has its privileges, its jurisdiction, its political rights, etc. It appears as the inorganic body of its lord. Hence the adage, *nulle terre sans maître*, in which the joint growth of lordship and landed property is expressed. The rule of landed property does not, therefore, appear as the direct rule of capital. Its dependants stand to it more in the relation in which they stand to their fatherland. It is a narrow kind of nationality.

[XVIII] Feudal landed property gives its name to its lord, as a kingdom gives its name to a king. His family history, the history of his house, etc., all this makes the landed property individual to him, makes it formally belong to a house, to a person. Similarly, the workers on the estate are not in the condition of *day-labourers*, but are partly the property of the lord, as in the case of serfs, and partly stand to him in relations of respect, subordination and duty. His relation to them is therefore directly political and has even an *agreeable* side. Customs and character differ from one estate to another and seem to be in harmony with the type of land, whereas later only a man's pocket, not his own character or individuality, attracts him to an estate. Finally, the lord does not try to extract the maximum profit from his estate. He rather consumes what is there, and tranquilly leaves the care of producing it to the serfs and tenant farmers. That is the *aristocratic* condition of land-ownership which reflects a romantic *glory* upon its lords.

It is inevitable that this appearance should be abolished, that landed property, the *root* of private property, should be drawn completely into the movement of private property and *become a commodity*; that the rule of the property owner should appear as the naked rule of private property, of capital, dissociated from all political colouring; that the relation between property owner and worker should be confined to the economic relationship of exploiter and exploited; that all personal relationships between the property owner and his property should cease, and the latter become purely *material* wealth; that in place of the honourable marriage with the land there should be a marriage of interest, and the land as well as man himself be reduced to the level of an object of speculation. It is inevitable that the root of landed property, sordid self-interest, should also appear in a cynical form. It is inevitable that immovable monopoly should turn into mobile and restless monopoly—into competition; and that the idle enjoyment of the products of other people's blood and toil should turn into a bustling trade in the same commodity. Finally, it is inevitable that in this competition, landed property, in the form of capital, should manifest its domination over both the working class and the property owners themselves, who are being ruined or advanced by the laws governing the movement of capital. So the medieval adage, *nulle terre sans seigneur*, is replaced with a new adage, *l'argent n'a pas de maître*, which expresses the complete domination of living men by dead matter.

[XIX] 2. As regards the controversy over the division or non-division of landed property, the following is to be observed.

The *division of landed property* negates the *large-scale monopoly* of landed property, i.e abolishes it, but only by *generalizing* it. It does not abolish the basis of monopoly, private property. It attacks the existence, but not the real essence, of monopoly, and in consequence it falls victim to the laws of private property. For the division of landed property corresponds to the movement of competition in the industrial sphere. This division of the implements of production and separation of labour (which must be carefully distinguished from the division of labour: the work is not divided among many individuals, but the same work is carried out by each individual; it is a multiplication of the same kind of work) does not only bring economic disadvantages; like all competition it leads to further accumulation.

When the division of landed property takes place, therefore, the only alternatives are to return to an even more hateful form of monopoly, or to negate and abolish the division of landed property itself. This latter course is not, however, a return to feudal property, but the abolition of private property in land altogether. The first supersession of monopoly is always an extension and generalization of it. The supersession of monopoly which has attained its widest and most inclusive existence is its complete destruction. Association, applied to the land, has the advantage from an economic point of view of large-scale ownership, while at the same time it realizes the original tendency of the division of land, namely equality. Moreover, association restores the intimate relationships between man and the land in a rational way, instead of through serfdom, overlordship and a foolish mystique of property. The land ceases to be an object of sordid speculation, and through the freedom of work and enjoyment becomes once more man's real personal property. One great advantage of the division of landed property is that the property of the masses is destroyed in a different way from that of industry, and they are no longer willing to accept serfdom.

As for the large estates, their defenders have always sophistically identified the economic advantages of large-scale agricultural production with the existence of large landed property, as if these advantages would not reach their greatest extent, and bring social benefits for the first time, with the abolition of private property. Similarly, they have attacked the commercial spirit of the small landowners, as though the large estates did not contain this petty trading in germ, even in their feudal form—not to speak of the modern English form in which the feudalism of landlords, and the trading and industry of tenant farmers, are combined.

Just as large landed property can return the reproach of monopoly made from the standpoint of small landholdings, since the division of land is also based upon the monopoly of private property, so can the small holdings reject the reproach of having divided the land, for the division of land exists also in the case of large estates, but in an inflexible, crystallized form. Private property, indeed, is everywhere based upon division. Moreover, since the division of landed property leads again to large landed property as capital wealth, feudal property is bound to be divided, or at least to fall into the hands of capitalists, however it may twist and turn.

For large landed property, as in England, drives the greater part of the industrial population into poverty and reduces its own workers to utter misery. It thus creates and augments the power of its enemies, capital and industry, so far as it thrusts the poor and a whole sphere of activity into the other camp. It makes the majority of the country industrial, and thus the enemy of large landed property. Where industry has attained considerable power, as at present in England, it opposes foreign monopolies to that of large landed property and forces the latter into competition with foreign landed property. Under the rule of industry, landed property could only maintain its feudal dimensions with the help of a monopoly against foreign countries, in order to protect itself against the universal laws of trade which contradict its feudal nature. Once thrown into competition it must conform with the laws of competition like any other commodity which is subject to them. But it becomes thereby so fluctuating, growing and diminishing, passing from hand to hand, that no law can keep it any longer in a few predestined hands. [XXI] The direct consequence is its fragmentation in many hands, a prey to the power of industrial capital.

In the end, large landed property which has been kept in existence by force and has created alongside itself a formidable industry, leads more rapidly to crisis than does the division of landed property alongside which the power of industry remains in second place.

As we can see in England, large landed property has cast off its feudal character and has taken on an industrial character to the extent that it wants to make as much money as possible. It gives the owner the highest possible rent, and the tenant farmer the highest possible profit on his capital. Consequently the agricultural workers are soon reduced to the minimum level of subsistence, and the farmer class establishes the power of industry and capital within landed property. Through competition with foreign countries the rent of land ceases, in the main, to constitute an independent source of income. A large section of the landowners is obliged to take the place of the tenant farmers who sink in this way into the proletariat. On the other hand, many tenant farmers will acquire landed property, for the large landowners, who have abandoned themselves to the enjoyment of their comfortable revenues and are usually unfitted for large-scale agricultural management, have very often neither the capital nor the experience to exploit the land.

Consequently, a section of them is completely ruined. Ultimately, the wages which have already been reduced to a minimum must be further reduced, in the face of new competition; and that leads necessarily to revolution.

Landed property had to develop in both these ways, in order to experience in both of them its inevitable decline. So also industry had to ruin itself both in the form of monopoly and in the form of competition, in order to arrive at faith in man.

ALIENATED LABOUR

[XXII] WE have begun from the presuppositions of political economy. We have accepted its terminology and its laws. We presupposed private property; the separation of labour, capital and land, as also of wages, profit and rent; the division of labour; competition; the concept of exchange value, etc. From political economy itself, in its own words, we have shown that the worker sinks to the level of a commodity, and to a most miserable commodity; that the misery of the worker increases with the power and volume of his production; that the necessary result of competition is the accumulation of capital in a few hands, and thus a restoration of monopoly in a more terrible form; and finally that the distinction between capitalist and landlord, and between agricultural labourer and industrial worker, must disappear, and the whole of society divide into the two classes of property *owners* and *propertyless* workers.

Political economy begins with the fact of private property; it does not explain it. It conceives the *material* process of private property, as this occurs in reality, in general and abstract formulas which then serve it as laws. It does not *comprehend* these laws; that is, it does not show how they arise out of the nature of private property. Political economy provides no explanation of the basis for the distinction of labour from capital, of capital from land. When, for example, the relation of wages to profits is defined, this is explained in terms of the interests of capitalists; in other words, what should be explained is assumed. Similarly, competition is referred to at every point and is explained in terms of external conditions. Political economy tells us nothing about the extent to which these external and apparently accidental conditions are simply the expression of a necessary development. We have seen how exchange itself seems an accidental fact. The only motive forces which political economy recognizes are *avarice* and the *war between the avaricious, competition.*

Just because political economy fails to understand the interconnexions within this movement it was possible to oppose the doctrine of competition to that of monopoly, the doctrine of freedom of the crafts to that of the guilds, the doctrine of the division of landed property to that of the great estates; for competition, freedom of crafts, and the division of landed property were conceived only as accidental consequences brought about by will and force, rather than as necessary, inevitable and natural consequences of monopoly, the guild system and feudal property.

Thus we have now to grasp the real connexion between this whole system of alienation—private property, acquisitiveness, the separation of labour, capital and land, exchange and competition, value and the devaluation of man, monopoly and competition—and the system of *money.*

Let us not begin our explanation, as does the economist, from a legendary primordial condition. Such a primordial condition does not explain anything; it merely removes the question into a grey and nebulous distance. It asserts as a fact or event what it should deduce, namely, the necessary relation between two things; for example, between the division of labour and exchange. In the same way theology explains the origin of evil by the fall of man; that is, it asserts as a historical fact what it should explain.

We shall begin from a *contemporary* economic fact. The worker becomes poorer the more wealth he produces and the more his production increases in power and extent. The worker becomes an ever cheaper commodity the more goods he creates. The *devaluation* of the human world increases in direct relation with the *increase in value* of the world of things. Labour does not only create goods; it also produces itself and the worker as a *commodity,* and indeed in the same proportion as it produces goods.

This fact simply implies that the object produced by labour, its product, now stands opposed to it as an *alien being*, as a *power independent* of the producer.   The product of labour is labour which has been embodied in an object and turned into a physical thing; this product is an *objectification* of labour.   The performance of work is at the same time its objectification.   The performance of work appears in the sphere of political economy as a *vitiation* of the worker, objectification as a *loss* and as *servitude to the object*, and appropriation as *alienation*.

So much does the performance of work appear as vitiation that the worker is vitiated to the point of starvation.   So much does objectification appear as loss of the object that the worker is deprived of the most essential things not only of life but also of work.   Labour itself becomes an object which he can acquire only by the greatest effort and with unpredictable interruptions.   So much does the appropriation of the object appear as alienation that the more objects the worker produces the fewer he can possess and the more he falls under the domination of his product, of capital.

All these consequences follow from the fact that the worker is related to the *product of his labour* as to an *alien* object.   For it is clear on this presupposition that the more the worker expends himself in work the more powerful becomes the world of objects which he creates in face of himself, the poorer he becomes in his inner life, and the less he belongs to himself.   It is just the same as in religion. The more of himself man attributes to God the less he has left in himself.   The worker puts his life into the object, and his life then belongs no longer to himself but to the object. The greater his activity, therefore, the less he possesses. What is embodied in the product of his labour is no longer his own.   The greater this product is, therefore, the more he is diminished.   The *alienation* of the worker in his product means not only that his labour becomes an object, assumes an *external* existence, but that it exists independently, *outside himself*, and alien to him, and that it stands opposed to him as an autonomous power. The life which he has given to the object sets itself against him as an alien and hostile force.

[XXIII] Let us now examine more closely the pheno-menon of *objectification*; the worker's production and the *alienation* and *loss* of the object it produces, which is involved in it. The worker can create nothing without *nature*, without the *sensuous external world*. The latter is the material in which his labour is realized, in which it is active, out of which and through which it produces things.

But just as nature affords the *means of existence* of labour, in the sense that labour cannot *live* without objects upon which it can be exercised, so also it provides the *means of existence* in a narrower sense; namely the means of physical existence for the *worker* himself. Thus, the more the worker *appro-priates* the external world of sensuous nature by his labour the more he deprives himself of *means of existence*, in two re-spects: first, that the sensuous external world becomes pro-gressively less an object belonging to his labour or a means of existence of his labour, and secondly, that it becomes pro-gressively less a means of existence in the direct sense, a means for the physical subsistence of the worker.

In both respects, therefore, the worker becomes a slave of the object; first, in that he receives an *object of work*, i.e. receives *work*, and secondly, in that he receives *means of sub-sistence*. Thus the object enables him to exist, first as a *worker* and secondly, as a *physical subject*. The culmination of this enslavement is that he can only maintain himself as a *physical subject* so far as he is a *worker*, and that it is only as a *physical subject* that he is a worker.

(The alienation of the worker in his object is expressed as follows in the laws of political economy: the more the worker produces the less he has to consume; the more value he creates the more worthless he becomes; the more refined his product the more crude and misshapen the worker; the more civilized the product the more barbarous the worker;

the more powerful the work the more feeble the worker; the more the work manifests intelligence the more the worker declines in intelligence and becomes a slave of nature.)

Political economy conceals the alienation in the nature of labour in so far as it does not examine the direct relationship between the worker (work) and production. Labour certainly produces marvels for the rich but it produces privation for the worker. It produces palaces, but hovels for the worker. It produces beauty, but deformity for the worker. It replaces labour by machinery, but it casts some of the workers back into a barbarous kind of work and turns the others into machines. It produces intelligence, but also stupidity and cretinism for the workers.

The direct relationship of labour to its products is the relationship of the worker to the objects of his production. The relationship of property owners to the objects of production and to production itself is merely a *consequence* of this first relationship and confirms it. We shall consider this second aspect later.

Thus, when we ask what is the important relationship of labour, we are concerned with the relationship of the *worker* to production.

So far we have considered the alienation of the worker only from one aspect; namely, *his relationship with the products of his labour.* However, alienation appears not merely in the result but also in the *process* of *production,* within *productive activity* itself. How could the worker stand in an alien relationship to the product of his activity if he did not alienate himself in the act of production itself? The product is indeed only the *résumé* of activity, of production. Consequently, if the product of labour is alienation, production itself must be active alienation—the alienation of activity and the activity of alienation. The alienation of the object of labour merely summarizes the alienation in the work activity itself.

What constitutes the alienation of labour? First, that the work is *external* to the worker, that it is not part of his nature;

and that, consequently, he does not fulfil himself in his work but denies himself, has a feeling of misery rather than well-being, does not develop freely his mental and physical energies but is physically exhausted and mentally debased. The worker, therefore, feels himself at home only during his leisure time, whereas at work he feels homeless. His work is not voluntary but imposed, *forced labour*. It is not the satisfaction of a need, but only a *means* for satisfying other needs. Its alien character is clearly shown by the fact that as soon as there is no physical or other compulsion it is avoided like the plague. External labour, labour in which man alienates himself, is a labour of self-sacrifice, of mortification. Finally, the external character of work for the worker is shown by the fact that it is not his own work but work for someone else, that in work he does not belong to himself but to another person.

Just as in religion the spontaneous activity of human fantasy, of the human brain and heart, reacts independently as an alien activity of gods or devils upon the individual, so the activity of the worker is not his own spontaneous activity. It is another's activity and a loss of his own spontaneity.

We arrive at the result that man (the worker) feels himself to be freely active only in his animal functions—eating, drinking and procreating, or at most also in his dwelling and in personal adornment—while in his human functions he is reduced to an animal. The animal becomes human and the human becomes animal.

Eating, drinking and procreating are of course also genuine human functions. But abstractly considered, apart from the environment of human activities, and turned into final and sole ends, they are animal functions.

We have now considered the act of alienation of practical human activity, labour, from two aspects: (1) the relationship of the worker to the *product of labour* as an alien object which dominates him. This relationship is at the same time the relationship to the sensuous external world, to natural objects, as an alien and hostile world; (2) the relationship of labour to the *act of production* within *labour*. This is the relationship of the worker to his own activity as something alien and not belonging to him, activity as suffering (passivity), strength as powerlessness, creation as emasculation, the *personal* physical and mental energy of the worker, his personal life (for what is life but activity?), as an activity which is directed against himself, independent of him and not belonging to him. This is *self-alienation* as against the above-mentioned alienation of the *thing*.

[XXIV] We have now to infer a third characteristic of *alienated labour* from the two we have considered.

Man is a species-being not only in the sense that he makes the community (his own as well as those of other things) his object both practically and theoretically, but also (and this is simply another expression for the same thing) in the sense that he treats himself as the present, living species, as a *universal* and consequently free being.[1]

Species-life, for man as for animals, has its physical basis in the fact that man (like animals) lives from inorganic nature, and since man is more universal than an animal so the range of inorganic nature from which he lives is more universal. Plants, animals, minerals, air, light, etc. constitute, from the theoretical aspect, a part of human consciousness as objects of natural science and art; they are man's spiritual inorganic nature, his intellectual means of life, which he must first prepare for enjoyment and perpetuation. So also, from the practical aspect, they form a part of human life and activity. In practice man lives only from these natural products, whether in the form of food, heating, clothing, housing, etc. The universality of man appears in practice in the universality which makes the whole of nature into his inorganic body: (1) as a direct means of life; and equally (2) as the material object and instrument of his life activity. Nature

[1] In this passage Marx reproduces Feuerbach's argument in *Das Wesen des Christentums*. *See* note 2 on p. 13 above. [*Editor's note.*]

is the inorganic body of man; that is to say nature, excluding the human body itself. To say that man *lives* from nature means that nature is his *body* with which he must remain in a continuous interchange in order not to die. The statement that the physical and mental life of man, and nature, are interdependent means simply that nature is interdependent with itself, for man is a part of nature.

Since alienated labour: (1) alienates nature from man; and (2) alienates man from himself, from his own active function, his life activity; so it alienates him from the species. It makes *species-life* into a means of individual life. In the first place it alienates species-life and individual life, and secondly, it turns the latter, as an abstraction, into the purpose of the former, also in its abstract and alienated form.

For labour, *life activity, productive life*, now appear to man only as *means* for the satisfaction of a need, the need to maintain his physical existence. Productive life is, however, species-life. It is life creating life. In the type of life activity resides the whole character of a species, its species-character; and free, conscious activity is the species-character of human beings. Life itself appears only as a *means of life*.

The animal is one with its life activity. It does not distinguish the activity from itself. It is *its activity*. But man makes his life activity itself an object of his will and consciousness. He has a conscious life activity. It is not a determination with which he is completely identified. Conscious life activity distinguishes man from the life activity of animals. Only for this reason is he a species-being. Or rather, he is only a self-conscious being, i.e. his own life is an object for him, because he is a species-being. Only for this reason is his activity free activity. Alienated labour reverses the relationship, in that man because he is a self-conscious being makes his life activity, his *being*, only a means for his *existence*.

The practical construction of an *objective world*, the

manipulation of inorganic nature, is the confirmation of man as a conscious species-being, i.e. a being who treats the species as his own being or himself as a species-being. Of course, animals also produce. They construct nests, dwellings, as in the case of bees, beavers, ants, etc. But they only produce what is strictly necessary for themselves or their young. They produce only in a single direction, while man produces universally. They produce only under the compulsion of direct physical needs, while man produces when he is free from physical need and only truly produces in freedom from such need. Animals produce only themselves, while man reproduces the whole of nature. The products of animal production belong directly to their physical bodies, while man is free in face of his product. Animals construct only in accordance with the standards and needs of the species to which they belong, while man knows how to produce in accordance with the standards of every species and knows how to apply the appropriate standard to the object. Thus man constructs also in accordance with the laws of beauty.

It is just in his work upon the objective world that man really proves himself as a *species-being*. This production is his active species-life. By means of it nature appears as *his* work and his reality. The object of labour is, therefore, the *objectification of man's species-life*; for he no longer reproduces himself merely intellectually, as in consciousness, but actively and in a real sense, and he sees his own reflection in a world which he has constructed. While, therefore, alienated labour takes away the object of production from man, it also takes away his *species-life*, his real objectivity as a species-being, and changes his advantage over animals into a disadvantage in so far as his inorganic body, nature, is taken from him.

Just as alienated labour transforms free and self-directed activity into a means, so it transforms the species-life of man into a means of physical existence.

Consciousness, which man has from his species, is transformed through alienation so that species-life becomes only a means for him. (3) Thus alienated labour turns the *species-life of man*, and also nature as his mental species-property, into an *alien* being and into a *means* for his *individual existence*. It alienates from man his own body, external nature, his mental life and his *human* life. (4) A direct consequence of the alienation of man from the product of his labour, from his life activity and from his species-life, is that *man* is *alienated* from other *men*. When man confronts himself he also confronts *other* men. What is true of man's relationship to his work, to the product of his work and to himself, is also true of his relationship to other men, to their labour and to the objects of their labour.

In general, the statement that man is alienated from his species-life means that each man is alienated from others, and that each of the others is likewise alienated from human life.

Human alienation, and above all the relation of man to himself, is first realized and expressed in the relationship between each man and other men. Thus in the relationship of alienated labour every man regards other men according to the standards and relationships in which he finds himself placed as a worker.

[XXV] We began with an economic fact, the alienation of the worker and his production. We have expressed this fact in conceptual terms as *alienated labour*, and in analysing the concept we have merely analysed an economic fact.

Let us now examine further how this concept of alienated labour must express and reveal itself in reality. If the product of labour is alien to me and confronts me as an alien power, to whom does it belong? If my own activity does not belong to me but is an alien, forced activity, to whom does it belong? To a being *other* than myself. And who is this being? The *gods*? It is apparent in the earliest stages of advanced production, e.g. temple building, etc. in Egypt, India, Mexico, and in the service rendered to gods, that the product belonged to the gods. But the gods alone were never the lords of labour. And no more was *nature*. What a contradiction it would be if the more man subjugates nature by his labour, and the more the marvels of the gods are rendered superfluous by the marvels of industry, the more he should abstain from his joy in producing and his enjoyment of the product for love of these powers.

The *alien* being to whom labour and the product of labour belong, to whose service labour is devoted, and to whose enjoyment the product of labour goes, can only be *man* himself. If the product of labour does not belong to the worker, but confronts him as an alien power, this can only be because it belongs to *a man other than the worker*. If his activity is a torment to him it must be a source of *enjoyment* and pleasure to another. Not the gods, nor nature, but only man himself can be this alien power over men.

Consider the earlier statement that the relation of man to himself is first *realized*, *objectified*, through his relation to other men. If he is related to the product of his labour, his objectified labour, as to an *alien*, hostile, powerful and independent object, he is related in such a way that another alien, hostile, powerful and independent man is the lord of this object. If he is related to his own activity as to unfree activity, then he is related to it as activity in the service, and under the domination, coercion and yoke, of another man.

Every self-alienation of man, from himself and from nature, appears in the relation which he postulates between other men and himself and nature. Thus religious self-alienation is necessarily exemplified in the relation between laity and priest, or, since it is here a question of the spiritual world, between the laity and a mediator. In the real world of practice this self-alienation can only be expressed in the real, practical relation of man to his fellow men. The medium through which alienation occurs is itself a *practical* one. Through alienated labour, therefore, man not only produces his relation to the object and to the process of production as

to alien and hostile men; he also produces the relation of
other men to his production and his product, and the relation
between himself and other men. Just as he creates his own
production as a vitiation, a punishment, and his own product
as a loss, as a product which does not belong to him, so he
creates the domination of the non-producer over production
and its product. As he alienates his own activity, so he
bestows upon the stranger an activity which is not his
own.

We have so far considered this relation only from the side
of the worker, and later on we shall consider it also from the
side of the non-worker.

Thus, through alienated labour the worker creates the
relation of another man, who does not work and is outside the
work process, to this labour. The relation of the worker to
work also produces the relation of the capitalist (or whatever
one likes to call the lord of labour) to work. *Private property*
is, therefore, the product, the necessary result, of *alienated
labour*, of the external relation of the worker to nature and to
himself.

Private property is thus derived from the analysis of the concept of *alienated labour*; that is, alienated man, alienated
labour, alienated life, and estranged man.

We have, of course, derived the concept of *alienated labour*
(*alienated life*) from political economy, from an analysis of the
movement of private property. But the analysis of this concept
shows that although private property appears to be the basis
and cause of alienated labour, it is rather a consequence of
the latter, just as the gods are *fundamentally* not the cause but
the product of confusions of human reason. At a later
stage, however, there is a reciprocal influence.

Only in the final stage of the development of private
property is its secret revealed, namely, that it is on one hand
the *product* of alienated labour, and on the other hand the
means by which labour is alienated, *the realization of this
alienation*.

This elucidation throws light upon several unresolved controversies—

1. Political economy begins with labour as the real soul of production and then goes on to attribute nothing to labour and everything to private property. Proudhon, faced by this contradiction, has decided in favour of labour against private property. We perceive, however, that this apparent contradiction is the contradiction of *alienated labour* with itself and that political economy has merely formulated the laws of alienated labour.

We also observe, therefore, that *wages* and *private property* are identical, for wages, like the product or object of labour, labour itself remunerated, are only a necessary consequence of the alienation of labour. In the wage system labour appears not as an end in itself but as the servant of wages. We shall develop this point later on and here only bring out some of the [XXVI] consequences.

An enforced *increase in wages* (disregarding the other difficulties, and especially that such an anomaly could only be maintained by force) would be nothing more than a *better remuneration of slaves*, and would not restore, either to the worker or to the work, their human significance and worth.

Even the *equality of incomes* which Proudhon demands would only change the relation of the present-day worker to his work into a relation of all men to work. Society would then be conceived as an abstract capitalist.

2. From the relation of alienated labour to private property it also follows that the emancipation of society from private property, from servitude, takes the political form of the *emancipation of the workers*; not in the sense that only the latter's emancipation is involved, but because this emancipation includes the emancipation of humanity as a whole. For all human servitude is involved in the relation of the worker to production, and all the types of

servitude are only modifications or consequences of this relation.

As we have discovered the concept of *private property* by an *analysis* of the concept of *alienated labour*, so with the aid of these two factors we can evolve all the *categories* of political economy, and in every category, e.g. trade, competition, capital, money, we shall discover only a particular and developed expression of these fundamental elements.

However, before considering this structure let us attempt to solve two problems.

1. To determine the general nature of *private property* as it has resulted from alienated labour, in its relation to *genuine human and social property*.

2. We have taken as a fact and analysed the *alienation of labour*. How does it happen, we may ask, that *man alienates his labour*? How is this alienation founded in the nature of human development? We have already done much to solve the problem in so far as we have *transformed* the question concerning the *origin of private property* into a question about the relation between *alienated labour* and the process of development of mankind. For in speaking of private property one believes oneself to be dealing with something external to mankind. But in speaking of labour one deals directly with mankind itself. This new formulation of the problem already contains its solution.

ad (1) *The general nature of private property and its relation to genuine human property.*

We have resolved alienated labour into two parts, which mutually determine each other, or rather, which constitute two different expressions of one and the same relation. *Appropriation* appears as *alienation* and *alienation* as *appropriation*, alienation as genuine acceptance in the community.

We have considered one aspect, *alienated* labour, in its bearing upon the *worker* himself, i.e. *the relation of alienated labour to itself.* And we have found as the necessary consequence of this relation the *property relation* of the *non-worker* to the *worker* and to labour. *Private property* as the material, summarized expression of alienated labour includes both relations; *the relation of the worker to labour, to the product of his labour and to the non-worker,* and the relation of the *non-worker to the worker and to the product of the latter's labour.*

We have already seen that in relation to the worker, who *appropriates* nature by his labour, appropriation appears as alienation, self-activity as activity for another and of another, living as the sacrifice of life, and production of the object as loss of the object to an alien power, an alien man. Let us now consider the relation of this *alien* man to the worker, to labour, and to the object of labour.

It should be noted first that everything which appears to the worker as an *activity of alienation,* appears to the non-worker as a *condition of alienation.* Secondly, the *real, practical* attitude (as a state of mind) of the worker in production and to the product appears to the non-worker who confronts him as a *theoretical* attitude.

[XXVII] Thirdly, the non-worker does everything against the worker which the latter does against himself, but he does not do against himself what he does against the worker.

Let us examine these three relationships more closely.[1]

---

[1] The manuscript breaks off unfinished at this point. [*Editor's note.*]

SECOND MANUSCRIPT

THE RELATIONSHIP OF PRIVATE PROPERTY

[XL] . . . forms the interest on his capital. The worker is the subjective manifestation of the fact that capital is man wholly lost to himself, just as capital is the objective manifestation of the fact that labour is man lost to himself. However, the *worker* has the misfortune to be a *living* capital, a capital with *needs*, which forfeits its interest and consequently its livelihood during every moment that it is not at work. As capital, the *value* of the worker varies according to supply and demand, and his *physical existence*, his *life*, was and is considered as a supply of goods, similar to any other goods. The worker produces capital and capital produces him. Thus he produces himself, and man as a *worker*, as a *commodity*, is the product of the whole process. Man is simply a *worker*, and as a worker his human qualities only exist for the sake of capital which is *alien* to him. Since labour and capital are alien to each other, and thus related only in an external and accidental manner, this alien character must *appear* in reality. As soon as it occurs to capital—either necessarily or voluntarily—not to exist any longer for the worker, he no longer exists for himself; he has *no* work, *no* wage, and since he exists only as a *worker* and not as a *human being*, he may as well let himself starve, be buried, etc. The worker is only a worker when he exists as capital *for himself*, and he only exists as capital when *capital* is there *for him*. The existence of capital is *his* existence, his life, since it determines the content of his life independently of him. Political economy thus does not recognize the unoccupied worker, the working man so far as he is outside this work relationship. Swindlers, thieves, beggars, the unemployed, the starving, poverty-stricken and criminal working man, are figures which do not exist for political economy, but only for other eyes; for doctors, judges, grave-diggers, beadles, etc. They are ghostly figures outside the domain of political economy. The needs of the worker are thus reduced to the need to maintain him *during work*, so that the race of workers does not die out. Consequently, wages have exactly the same significance as the *maintenance* of any other productive instrument, and as the *consumption of capital* in general so that it can reproduce itself with interest. They are like the oil which is applied to a wheel to keep it running. Wages thus form part of the necessary *costs* of capital and of the capitalist, and they must not exceed this necessary amount. Thus it was quite logical for the English factory lords, before the Amendment Bill of 1834, to deduct from the wages which they themselves paid, the public alms which workers received from the poor-law taxes, i.e. to treat public alms as an integral part of total wages.

Production does not only produce man as a *commodity*, the *human commodity*, man in the form of a *commodity*; in con-formity with this situation it produces him as a *mentally* and *physically* dehumanized being. . . . Immorality, miscarriage, helotism of workers and capitalists. . . . Its product is the *self-conscious* and *self-acting commodity*. . . . The *human* com-modity. . . . It is a great step forward by Ricardo, Mill, *et al.*, as against Smith and Say, to declare the *existence of* human beings—the greater or lesser human productivity of the commodity—as *indifferent* or indeed harmful. The true end of production is not the number of workers a given capital maintains, but the amount of interest it earns, the total annual saving. It was likewise a great and logical advance in recent [XLI] English political economy that, while establishing *labour* as the only principle of political economy, it clearly distinguished the inverse relation between wages and interest on capital, and observed that as a rule the capitalist could *only* increase his gains by the depression of wages and vice versa. The *normal* relation is seen to be not the defrauding of the consumer, but the mutual cheating of capitalist and worker. The relation of private property includes within itself, in a latent state, the relation of private property as labour, the relation of private property as capital, and the mutual influence of these two. On the one hand, there is the production of human activity as *labour*, that is, as an activity which is alien to itself, to man and to nature, and thus alien to consciousness and to the realization of human life; the abstract existence of man as a mere *working man*, who, therefore, plunges every day from his fulfilled nothingness into absolute nothingness, into social, and thus real, non-existence. On the other hand, there is the production of objects of human labour as *capital*, in which every natural and social characteristic of the object is *dissolved*, in which private property has lost its natural and social quality (and has thereby lost all political and social disguise and no longer even *appears* to be connected with human relationships), and in which the *same* capital remains the *same* in the most varied natural and social conditions, which have no relevance to its *real* content. This contradiction, at its highest point, is necessarily the summit and the point of decline of the whole relation.

It is, therefore, another great achievement of recent English political economy to have defined ground rent as the difference between the returns on the worst and the best cultivated land, to have demolished the romantic illusions of the landowner—his alleged social importance and the identity of his interests with those of society at large (a view which Adam Smith held even after the Physiocrats)—and to have anticipated and prepared the development in reality, which will transform the landowner into an ordinary, prosaic capitalist and thereby simplify the contradiction, bring it to a head and prepare its solution. *Land as land*, *ground rent as ground rent*, have lost their distinctive status and have become dumb *capital* and *interest*, or rather, capital and interest which only talk money.

The *distinction* between capital and land, profit and ground rent, and the distinction of both from wages, *industry, agriculture, immovable* and *movable* private property, is a *historical* distinction, not one inscribed in the nature of things. It is a *fixed* stage in the formation and development of the antithesis between capital and labour. In industry, etc., as opposed to immovable landed property, only the mode of origin and the antithesis to agriculture through which industry has developed, is expressed. As a *particular* kind of labour, as a more *significant, important* and *comprehensive* distinction, it exists only so long as industry (town life) is established *in opposition to* landed property (aristocratic feudal life) and still bears the characteristics of this contradiction in itself in the form of monopolies, crafts, guilds, corporations, etc. In such a situation, labour still appears to have a *social* meaning, still has the significance of *genuine* communal life, and has not yet progressed to *neutrality* in relation to its content, to full self-sufficient being, i.e. to abstraction from all other existence and thus to *liberated* capital.

[LXII] But the necessary *development* of labour is liberated *industry*, constituted for itself alone, and *liberated capital*. The power of industry over its opponent is shown by the rise of *agriculture* as a real industry, whereas formerly most of the work was left to the soil itself and to the *slave* of the soil through whom the land cultivated itself. With the transformation of the slave into a *free* worker, i.e. into a *hireling*, the landowner himself is transformed into a lord of industry, a capitalist.

This transformation takes place at first through the medium of the tenant farmer. But the tenant is the representative, the revealed *secret*, of the landowner. Only through him does the landowner have an *economic* existence, existence as a property owner; for the ground rent of his land only exists as a result of the competition between tenants. Thus the landowner *has* already become to a large extent, in the person of the tenant farmer, a *common* capitalist. And this must be fulfilled in reality; the capitalist directing agriculture (the tenant) must become a landowner, or vice versa. The *industrial trade* of the tenant is that of the landowner, for the existence of the former establishes that of the latter.

Recollecting their contrasting origins and descent the landowner recognizes the capitalist as his insubordinate, liberated and enriched slave of yesterday, and sees himself as a *capitalist* who is threatened by him. The capitalist sees the landowner as the idle, cruel and egoistical lord of yesterday; he knows that as a capitalist he injures the landowner, and yet that industry is responsible for the latter's present social significance, for his possessions and pleasures. He regards the landowner as the antithesis of *free* enterprise and of *free* capital which is independent of every natural limitation. This opposition is extremely bitter and each side expresses the truth about the other. It is only necessary to read the attacks upon immovable property by representatives of movable property, and vice versa, in order to obtain a clear picture of their respective worthlessness. The landowner emphasizes the noble lineage of his property, feudal souvenirs, reminiscences, the poetry of remembrance, his open-hearted character, his political importance, etc., and when he talks in economic terms asserts that agriculture *alone* is productive. At the same time he portrays his opponent as a sly, bargaining, deceitful, mercenary, rebellious, heartless and soulless individual, an extortionate, pimping, servile, smooth, flattering, desiccated rogue, without honour, principles, poetry or anything else, who is alienated from the community which he freely trades away, and who breeds, nourishes and cherishes competition and along with it poverty, crime and the dissolution of all social bonds. (*See* among others the Physiocrat, Bergasse, whom Camille Desmoulins scourged in his journal *Révolutions de France et de*

Brabant; *see also* von Vincke, Lancizolle, Haller, Leo,[1] Kosegarten and Sismondi.) [2]

Movable property, for its part, points to the miracle of modern industry and development. It is the child, the legitimate, native-born son, of the modern age. It pities its opponent as a simpleton, *ignorant* of his own nature (and this is entirely true) who wishes to replace moral capital and free labour by crude, immoral coercion and serfdom. It depicts him as a Don Quixote who, beneath the appearance of *directness*, *decency*, the *general interest* and stability, conceals his incapacity for development, greedy self-indulgence, selfishness, sectional interest and evil intention. It exposes him as a cunning *monopolist*; it pours cold water upon his reminiscences, his poetry and his romanticism, by a historical and satirical recital of the baseness, cruelty, degradation, prostitution, infamy, anarchy and revolt, of which the romantic castles were the workshops.

It (movable property) claims to have won political freedom for the people, to have removed the chains which bound civil society, to have linked together different worlds, to have established commerce which promotes friendship between peoples, to have created a pure morality and an agreeable culture. It has given the people, in place of their crude wants, civilized needs and the means of satisfying them. But the landowner—this idle speculator

---

[1] *See* the pompous Old-Hegelian theologian Funke who, according to Herr Leo, related with tears in his eyes how a slave had refused, when serfdom was abolished, to cease being a *noble possession*. *See also* JUSTUS MÖSER's *Patriotische Phantasien*, which are distinguished by the fact that they never for a moment abandon the ingenuous, petty-bourgeois, "home-made," ordinary, limited horizon of the philistine, and yet remain pure fantasy. It is this contradiction which has made them so attractive to the German mind.

[2] Here, and in his footnote, Marx refers especially to the following writings: CAMILLE DESMOULINS, *Révolutions de France et de Brabant*. Second trimestre contenant mars, avril, mai. Paris, l'an Ier. No. 16, p. 139 *et seq.*; No. 23, p. 425 *et seq.*; No. 26, p. 580 *et seq.* G. L. W. FUNKE, *Die aus der unbeschränkten Teilbarkeit des Grundeigentums hervorgehenden Nachteile*, Hamburg and Gotha 1829, quoted by HEINRICH LEO, *Studien und Skizzen zu einer Naturlehre des Staats*. 1 Abt. Halle 1833. JUSTUS MÖSER, *Patriotische Phantasien*. Berlin 1775-8. J. C. L. SIMONDE DE SISMONDI, op. cit. [*Editor's note.*]

in grain—raises the price of the people's basic necessities of life and thereby forces the capitalist to raise wages without being able to increase productivity, thus hindering and ultimately arresting the growth of national income and the accumulation of capital upon which depends the creation of work for the people and of wealth for the country. He brings about a general decline, and parasitically exploits *all* the advantages of modern civilization without making the least contribution to it, and without abandoning any of his feudal prejudices. Finally, let him—for whom cultivation and the land itself exist only as a heaven-sent source of money—regard the *tenant farmer* and say whether he himself is not a *straightforward, fantastic, cunning* scoundrel, who in his heart and in reality has long been captivated by *free* industry and by the *delights* of trade, however much he may resist them and prattle about historical reminiscences or moral and political aims. Everything which he can really bring forward in justification is true only of the *cultivator of the land* (the capitalist and the labourers) of whom the landowner is rather the *enemy*; thus he testifies against himself. *Without* capital, landed property is lifeless and worthless matter. It is indeed the civilized victory of movable property to have discovered and created human labour as the source of wealth, in place of the lifeless thing. (*See* Paul Louis Courier, Saint-Simon, Ganilh, Ricardo, Mill, MacCulloch, Destutt de Tracy, and Michel Chevalier.)

From the *real* course of development (to be inserted here) there follows the necessary victory of the capitalist, i.e. of developed private property, over undeveloped, immature private property, the landowner. In general, movement must triumph over immobility, overt self-conscious baseness over concealed, unconscious baseness, *avarice* over *self-indulgence*, the avowedly restless and able self-interest of *enlightenment* over the local, worldly-wise, simple, idle and fantastic *self-interest of superstition*, and *money* over the other forms of private property.

The states which have a presentiment of the danger represented by fully developed free industry, pure morality, and trade which promotes the amity of peoples, attempt, but quite in vain, to arrest the capitalization of landed property.

Landed property, as distinct from capital, is private property, capital, which is still afflicted by local and political prejudices; it is capital which has not yet emerged from its involvement with the world, *undeveloped* capital. In the course of its *formation on a world scale* it must achieve its abstract, i.e. *pure* expression.

The relations of private property are capital, labour and their interconnexions.

The movements through which these elements have to go are—

First—*unmediated* and *mediated unity of the two*. Capital and labour are at first still united; later indeed separated and alienated, but reciprocally developing and promoting each other as *positive* conditions.

Opposition between the two—they mutually exclude each other; the worker recognizes the capitalist as his own non-existence and vice versa; each seeks to rob the other of his existence.

Opposition of each *to* itself. Capital = accumulated labour = labour. As such it divides into *capital itself* and *interest*; the latter divides into *interest* and *profit*. Complete sacrifice of the capitalist. He sinks into the working class, just as the worker—but only exceptionally—becomes a capitalist. Labour as a moment of capital, its *costs*. Thus wages a sacrifice of capital.

Labour divides into *labour itself* and *wages of labour*. The worker himself a capital, a commodity.

Clash of reciprocal contradictions.[1]

---

[1] The second manuscript ends here. [*Editor's note.*]

THIRD MANUSCRIPT

PRIVATE PROPERTY AND LABOUR

[I] *ad* page XXXVI. The subjective essence of *private* property, private property as activity for itself, as *subject*, as *person*, is labour. It is evident, therefore, that only the political economy which recognized labour as its principle (Adam Smith) and which no longer regarded private property as merely a *condition* external to man, can be considered as both a product of the real *dynamism* and *development* of private property,[1] a product of modern *industry*, and a force which has accelerated and extolled the dynamism and development of industry and has made it a power in the domain of *consciousness*.

Thus, from the viewpoint of this enlightened political economy which has discovered the *subjective* essence of wealth within the framework of private property, the partisans of the monetary system and the mercantilist system, who consider private property as a *purely objective* being for man, are *fetishists* and *Catholics*. Engels is right, therefore, in calling Adam Smith the *Luther of political economy*. Just as Luther recognized religion and *faith* as the essence of the real *world*, and for that reason took up a position against Catholic paganism; just as he annulled *external* religiosity while making religiosity the *inner* essence of man; just as he negated the distinction between priest and layman because he transferred the priest into the heart of the layman; so wealth external to man and independent of him (and thus only to be acquired and conserved from outside) is annulled. That is to say, its *external* and *mindless objectivity* is annulled by the fact that private property is incorporated in man himself, and man himself is recognized as its essence. But as a result, man himself is brought into the sphere of private property,

[1] It is the independent movement of private property become conscious of itself; modern industry as Self.

147

just as, with Luther, he is brought into the sphere of religion. Under the guise of recognizing man, political economy, whose principle is labour, carries to its logical conclusion the denial of man.   Man himself is no longer in a condition of external tension with the external substance of private property; he has himself become the tension-ridden being of private property.   What was previously a phenomenon of *being external to oneself*, a real external manifestation of man, has now become the act of objectification, of alienation. This political economy seems at first, therefore, to recognize man with his independence, his personal activity, etc.   It incorporates private property in the very essence of man, and it is no longer, therefore, conditioned by the local or national *characteristics of private property* regarded as existing outside itself.   It manifests a cosmopolitan, universal activity which is destructive of every limit and every bond, and substitutes itself as the *only* policy, the *only* universality, the *only* limit and the *only* bond.   But in its further development it is obliged to discard this hypocrisy and to show itself in all its cynicism. It does this, without any regard for the apparent contradictions to which its doctrine leads, by showing in a more one-sided fashion, and thus with greater logic and clarity, that *labour* is the sole *essence of wealth*, and by demonstrating that this doctrine, in contrast with the original conception, has consequences which are *inimical to man*.   Finally, it gives the death-blow to *ground rent*; that last individual and natural form of private property and source of wealth existing independently of the movement of labour, which was the expression of feudal property but has become entirely its economic expression and is no longer able to put up any resistance to political economy.   (The Ricardo School.) Not only does the *cynicism* of political economy increase from Smith, through Say, to Ricardo, Mill, *et al.* inasmuch as for the latter the consequence of *industry* appeared more and more developed and contradictory; from a positive point of view they become more alienated, and more consciously alienated, from man, in comparison with their predecessors. This is *only* because their science develops with greater logic and truth. Since they make private property in its active form the subject, and since at the same time they make man as a non-being into a being, the contradiction in reality corresponds entirely with the contradictory essence which they have accepted as a principle. The divided [II] *reality* of *industry* is far from refuting, but instead confirms, its *self-divided* principle. Its principle is in fact the principle of this division.

The physiocratic doctrine of Quesnay forms the transition from the mercantilist system to Adam Smith. *Physiocracy* is in a direct sense the *economic* decomposition of feudal property, but for this reason it is equally directly the *economic transformation*, the re-establishment, of this same feudal property; with the difference that its language is no longer feudal but economic. All wealth is reduced to *land* and *cultivation* (agriculture). Land is not yet *capital* but is still a particular mode of existence of capital, whose value is claimed to reside in, and derive from, its natural particularity; but land is none the less a natural and universal *element*, whereas the mercantilist system regarded only precious metals as wealth. The object of wealth, its matter, has, therefore, been given the greatest universality within natural limits—inasmuch as it is also, as nature, directly objective wealth. And it is only by labour, by agriculture, that land exists for man. Consequently, the subjective essence of wealth is already transferred to labour. But at the same time agriculture is the *only productive labour*. Labour is, therefore, not yet taken in its universality and its abstract form; it is still bound to a particular *element of nature as its matter*, and is only recognized in a particular *mode of existence determined by nature*. Labour is still only a *determinate, particular* alienation of man, and its product is also conceived as a determinate part of wealth due more to nature than to labour itself. Land is still regarded here as something which exists naturally and independently of man, and not yet as capital, i.e. as a factor of labour. On the contrary, labour appears to be a factor of *nature*. But since the fetishism of the old external wealth, existing only as an object, has been reduced to a very simple natural element, and since its essence has been partially, and in a certain way, recognized in its subjective existence, the necessary advance has been made in recognizing the *universal nature* of wealth and in raising *labour* in its absolute form, i.e. in abstraction, to the *principle*. It is demonstrated against the Physiocrats that from the economic point of view (i.e. from the only valid point of view) agriculture does not differ from any other industry; and that it is not, therefore, a specific kind of labour, bound to a particular element, or a particular manifestation of labour, but *labour in general* which is the *essence* of wealth.

Physiocracy denies *specific*, external, purely objective wealth, in declaring that labour is its essence. For the Physiocrats, however, labour is in the first place only the *subjective essence* of landed property. (They begin from that kind of property which appears historically as the predominant recognized type.) They merely turn landed property into alienated man. They annul its feudal character by declaring that *industry* (agriculture) is its *essence*; but they reject the industrial world and accept the feudal system by declaring that *agriculture* is the only industry.

It is evident that when the *subjective essence*—industry in opposition to landed property, industry forming itself as industry—is grasped, this essence includes within itself the opposition. For just as industry incorporates the superseded landed property, its subjective essence incorporates the subjective essence of the latter.

Landed property is the first form of private property, and industry first appears historically in simple opposition to it, as a particular form of private property (or rather, as the liberated slave of landed property); this sequence is repeated in the scientific study of the *subjective* essence of private property, and labour appears at first only as *agricultural labour* but later establishes itself as *labour in general*.

[III] All wealth has become *industrial wealth*, the *wealth* of labour, and *industry* is realized labour; just as the *factory system* is the realized essence of *industry* (i.e. of labour), and as *industrial capital* is the realized objective form of private property. Thus we see that it is only at this stage that private property can consolidate its rule over man and become, in its most general form, a world-historical power.

PRIVATE PROPERTY AND COMMUNISM

ad page XXXIX. But the antithesis between *propertylessness* and *property* is still an indeterminate antithesis, which is not conceived in its *active reference* to its intrinsic relations, not yet conceived as a contradiction, so long as it is not understood as an antithesis between *labour* and *capital*. Even without the advanced development of private property, e.g. in ancient Rome, in Turkey, etc. this antithesis may be expressed in a primitive form. In this form it does not yet *appear* as established by private property itself. But labour, the subjective essence of private property as the exclusion of property, and capital, objective labour as the exclusion of labour, constitute *private property* as the developed relation of the contradiction and thus a dynamic relation which drives towards its resolution.

ad ibidem. The supersession of self-estrangement follows the same course as self-estrangement. *Private property* is first considered only from its objective aspect, but with labour conceived as its essence. Its mode of existence is, therefore, *capital* which it is necessary to abolish " as such " (Proudhon). Or else the *specific form* of labour (labour which is brought to a common level, subdivided, and thus unfree) is regarded as the source of the *nocivity* of private property and of its existence alienated from man. Fourier, in accord with the Physiocrats, regards *agricultural labour* as being at least the exemplary kind of labour. Saint-Simon asserts on the contrary that *industrial labour* as such is the essence of labour, and consequently he desires the *exclusive* rule of the industrialists and an amelioration of the condition of the workers. Finally, *communism* is the positive expression of the abolition of private property, and in the first place of universal private property. In taking this relation in its *universal aspect* communism is, in its first form, only the generalization and fulfilment of the relation. As such it appears in a double form; the domination of material property looms so large that it aims to destroy everything which is incapable of being possessed by everyone as private property. It wishes to eliminate talent, etc. by *force*. Immediate physical possession seems to it the unique goal of life and existence. The role of *worker* is not abolished, but is extended to all men. The relation of private property remains the relation of the community to the world of things. Finally, this tendency to oppose general private property to private property is expressed in an animal form; *marriage* (which is incontestably a form of *exclusive private property*) is contrasted with the community of women, in which women become communal and common property. One may say that this idea of the *community of women* is the *open secret* of this entirely crude and unreflective communism. Just as women are to pass from marriage to universal prostitution, so the whole world of wealth (i.e. the objective being of man) is to pass from the relation of exclusive marriage with the private owner to the relation of universal prostitution with the community. This communism, which negates the *personality* of man in every sphere, is only the logical expression of private property, which is this negation. Universal *envy* setting itself up as a power is only a camouflaged form of cupidity which re-establishes itself and satisfies itself in a different way. The thoughts of every individual private property are *at least* directed against any *wealthier* private property, in the form of envy and the desire to reduce everything to a common level; so that this envy and levelling in fact constitute the essence of competition. Crude communism is only the culmination of such envy and levelling-down on the basis of a *preconceived* minimum. How little this abolition of private property represents a genuine appropriation is shown by the abstract negation of the whole world of culture and civilization, and the regression to the *unnatural* [IV] simplicity of the poor and wantless individual who has not only not surpassed private property but has not yet even attained to it.

The community is only a community of *work* and of *equality of wages* paid out by the communal capital, by the *community* as universal capitalist. The two sides of the relation are raised to a *supposed* universality; *labour* as a condition in which everyone is placed, and *capital* as the acknowledged universality and power of the community.

In the relationship with *woman*, as the prey and the hand-maid of communal lust, is expressed the infinite degradation in which man exists for himself; for the secret of this relationship finds its *unequivocal*, incontestable, *open* and revealed expression in the relation of man to woman and in the way in which the *direct* and *natural* species-relationship is conceived. The immediate, natural and necessary relation of human being to human being is also the *relation* of *man* to *woman*. In this *natural* species-relationship man's relation to nature is directly his relation to man, and his relation to man is directly his relation to nature, to his own *natural* function. Thus, in this relation is *sensuously revealed*, reduced to an observable *fact*, the extent to which human nature has become nature for man and to which nature has become human nature for him. From this relationship man's whole level of development can be assessed. It follows from the character of this relationship how far *man* has become, and has understood himself as, a *species-being*, a *human being*. The relation of man to woman is the *most natural* relation of human being to human being. It indicates, therefore, how far man's *natural* behaviour has become *human*, and how far his *human* essence has become a *natural* essence for him, how far his *human nature* has become *nature* for him. It also shows how far man's needs have become *human* needs, and consequently how far the other person, as a person, has become one of his needs, and to what extent he is in his individual existence at the same time a social being. The first positive annulment of private property, crude communism, is, therefore, only a *phenomenal form* of the infamy of private property representing itself as positive community.

2. Communism (*a*) still political in nature, democratic or despotic; (*b*) with the abolition of the state, yet still incomplete and influenced by private property, that is, by the alienation of man. In both forms communism is already aware of being the reintegration of man, his return to himself, the supersession of man's self-alienation. But since it has not yet grasped the positive nature of private property, or the *human* nature of needs, it is still captured and contaminated by private property. It has well understood the concept, but not the essence.

3. *Communism* is the *positive* abolition of *private property*, of *human self-alienation*, and thus the real *appropriation* of *human* nature through and for man. It is, therefore, the return of man himself as a *social*, i.e. really human, being, a complete and conscious return which assimilates all the wealth of previous development. Communism as a fully developed naturalism is humanism and as a fully developed humanism is naturalism. It is the *definitive* resolution of the antagonism between man and nature, and between man and man. It is the true solution of the conflict between existence and essence, between objectification and self-affirmation, between freedom and necessity, between individual and species. It is the solution of the riddle of history and knows itself to be this solution.

[V] Thus the whole historical development, both the *real* genesis of communism (the birth of its empirical existence) and its thinking consciousness, is its comprehended and conscious process of becoming; whereas the other, still undeveloped, communism seeks in certain historical forms opposed to private property a *historical* justification founded upon what already exists, and to this end tears out of their context isolated elements of this development (Cabet [1] and

---

[1] ETIENNE CABET (1788–1856); author of *Voyage en Icarie* (1840) and founder of a Utopian Community, Icaria, in Illinois. [*Editor's note.*]

Villegardelle are pre-eminent among those who ride this hobby-horse) and asserts them as proofs of its historical pedigree. In doing so, it makes clear that by far the greater part of this development contradicts its own assertions, and that if it has ever existed its past existence refutes its pretension to *essential being*.

It is easy to understand the necessity which leads the whole revolutionary movement to find its empirical, as well its as theoretical, basis in the development of *private property*, and more precisely of the economic system.

This material, directly *perceptible* private property is the material and sensuous expression of *alienated human* life. Its movement—production and consumption—is the *sensuous* manifestation of the movement of all previous production, i.e. the realization or reality of man. Religion, the family, the state, law, morality, science, art, etc. are only *particular* forms of production and come under its general law. The positive supersession of *private property*, as the appropriation of *human* life, is, therefore, the positive supersession of all alienation, and the return of man from religion, the family, the state, etc. to his *human*, i.e. social life. Religious alienation as such occurs only in the sphere of *consciousness*, in the inner life of man, but economic alienation is that of *real life* and its supersession, therefore, affects both aspects. Of course, the development in different nations has a different beginning according to whether the actual and *established* life of the people is more in the realm of mind or more in the external world, is a real or ideal life. Communism begins where atheism begins (Owen), but atheism is at the outset still far from being *communism*; indeed it is still for the most part an abstraction.[1]

---

[1] Marx inserted a note here which referred back to his discussion of " crude communism ": " Prostitution is only a *specific* expression of the *universal* prostitution of the worker, and since prostitution is a relationship which includes both the one who is prostituted and the one who prostitutes (and the latter is much more base), so the capitalist, etc. comes within this category." [*Editor's note.*]

Thus the philanthropy of atheism is at first only an abstract *philosophical* philanthropy, whereas that of communism is at once *real* and oriented towards *action*.

We have seen how, on the assumption that private property has been positively superseded, man produces man, himself and then other men; how the object which is the direct activity of his personality is at the same time his existence for other men and their existence for him. Similarly, the material of labour and man himself as a subject are the starting-point as well as the result of this movement (and because there must be this starting-point private property is a historical necessity). Therefore, the *social* character is the universal character of the whole movement; *as* society itself produces *man* as *man*, so it is *produced* by him. Activity and mind are social in their content as well as in their *origin*; they are *social* activity and social mind. The *human* significance of nature only exists for *social* man, because only in this case is nature a *bond* with other *men*, the basis of his existence for others and of their existence for him. Only then is nature the *basis* of his own *human* experience and a vital element of human reality. The *natural* existence of man has here become his *human* existence and nature itself has become human for him. Thus *society* is the accomplished union of man with nature, the veritable resurrection of nature, the realized naturalism of man and the realized humanism of nature.

[VI] Social activity and social mind by no means exist *only* in the form of activity or mind which is directly communal. Nevertheless, communal activity and mind, i.e. activity and mind which express and confirm themselves directly in a *real association* with other men, occur everywhere where this direct expression of sociability arises from the content of the activity or corresponds to the nature of mind.

Even when I carry out *scientific* work, etc., an activity which I can seldom conduct in direct association with other men, I perform a *social*, because *human*, act. It is not only the material of my activity—such as the language itself which the thinker uses—which is given to me as a social product. My *own existence* is a social activity. For this reason, what I myself produce I produce for society, and with the consciousness of acting as a social being.

My universal consciousness is only the *theoretical* form of that whose *living* form is the real community, the social entity, although at the present day this universal consciousness is an abstraction from real life and is opposed to it as an enemy. That is why the *activity* of my universal consciousness as such is my *theoretical* existence as a social being.

It is above all necessary to avoid postulating " society " once again as an abstraction confronting the individual. The individual *is* the *social being*. The manifestation of his life—even when it does not appear directly in the form of a communal manifestation, accomplished in association with other men—is, therefore, a manifestation and affirmation of *social life*. Individual human life and species-life are not different things, even though the mode of existence of individual life is necessarily either a more *specific* or a more *general* mode of species-life, or that of species-life a *specific* or more *general* mode of individual life.

In his *species-consciousness* man confirms his real *social life*, and reproduces his real existence in thought; while conversely, species-life confirms itself in species-consciousness and exists for itself in its universality as a thinking being. Though man is a unique individual—and it is just his particularity which makes him an individual, a really *individual* communal being—he is equally the *whole*, the ideal whole, the subjective existence of society as thought and experienced. He exists in reality as the representation and the real mind of social existence, and as the sum of human manifestations of life.

Thought and being are indeed *distinct* but they also form a unity. *Death* seems to be a harsh victory of the species over the individual and to contradict their unity; but the particular individual is only a *determinate species-being* and as such he is mortal.

4. Just as *private property* is only the sensuous expression of the fact that man is at the same time an *objective* fact for himself and becomes an alien and non-human object for himself; just as his manifestation of life is also his alienation of life and his self-realization a loss of reality, the emergence of an *alien* reality; so the positive supersession of private property, i.e. the *sensuous* appropriation of the human essence and of human life, of objective man and of human *creations*, by and for man, should not be taken only in the sense of *immediate*, exclusive *enjoyment*, or only in the sense of *possession* or *having*. Man appropriates his manifold being in an all-inclusive way, and thus as a whole man. All his *human* relations to the world—seeing, hearing, smelling, tasting, touching, thinking, observing, feeling, desiring, acting, loving—in short, all the organs of his individuality, like the organs which are directly communal in form, [VII] are in their objective action (their *action in relation to the object*) the appropriation of this object, the appropriation of human reality. The way in which they react to the object is the confirmation of *human reality*.[1] It is human effectiveness and human *suffering*, for suffering humanly considered is an enjoyment of the self for man.

Private property has made us so stupid and partial that an object is only *ours* when we have it, when it exists for us as capital or when it is directly eaten, drunk, worn, inhabited, etc., in short, *utilized* in some way. But private property itself only conceives these various forms of possession as *means of life*, and the life for which they serve as means is the *life* of *private property*—labour and creation of capital.

Thus *all* the physical and intellectual senses have been replaced by the simple alienation of *all* these senses; the

[1] It is, therefore, just as varied as the determinations of human nature and activities are diverse.

sense of *having*. The human being had to be reduced to this absolute poverty in order to be able to give birth to all his inner wealth. (On the category of *having* see Hess in *Einundzwanzig Bogen*.) [1]

The supersession of private property is, therefore, the complete *emancipation* of all the human qualities and senses. It is such an emancipation because these qualities and senses have become *human*, from the subjective as well as the objective point of view. The eye has become a *human* eye when its *object* has become a *human*, social object, created by man and destined for him. The senses have, therefore, become directly theoreticians in practice. They relate themselves to the thing for the sake of the thing, but the thing itself is an *objective human* relation to itself and to man, and vice versa. [2] Need and enjoyment have thus lost their *egoistic* character and nature has lost its mere *utility* by the fact that its utilization has become *human* utilization.

Similarly, the senses and minds of other men have become my *own* appropriation. Thus besides these direct organs, *social* organs are constituted, in the form of society; for example, activity in direct association with others has become an organ for the manifestation of life and a mode of appropriation of *human* life.

It is evident that the human eye appreciates things in a different way from the crude, non-human eye, the human *ear* differently from the crude ear. As we have seen, it is only when the object becomes a *human* object, or objective *humanity*, that man does not become lost in it. This is only possible when man himself becomes a *social* object; when he himself becomes a social being and society becomes a being for him in this object.

On the one hand, it is only when objective reality everywhere becomes for man in society the reality of human

---

[1] *Einundzwanzig Bogen aus der Schweiz*, op. cit., p. 329.
[2] In practice I can only relate myself in a human way to a thing when the thing is related in a human way to man.

faculties, human reality, and thus the reality of his own faculties, that all *objects* become for him the *objectification of himself.* The objects then confirm and realize his individuality, they are *his own* objects, i.e. man himself becomes the object. *The manner in which these objects* become his own depends upon the *nature of the object* and the nature of the corresponding faculty; for it is precisely the *determinate character* of this relation which constitutes the specific *real* mode of affirmation. The object is not the same for the *eye* as for the *ear*, for the ear as for the eye. The *distinctive character* of each faculty is precisely its *characteristic* essence and thus also the characteristic mode of its objectification, of its *objectively real*, living *being.* It is therefore not only in thought, [VIII] but through *all* the senses that man is affirmed in the objective world.

Let us next consider the subjective aspect. Man's musical sense is only awakened by music. The most beautiful music has no meaning for the non-musical ear, is not an object for it, because my object can only be the confirmation of one of my own faculties. It can only be so for me in so far as my faculty exists for itself as a subjective capacity, because the meaning of an object for me extends only as far as the sense extends (only makes sense for an appropriate sense). For this reason, the *senses* of social man are *different* from those of non-social man. It is only through the objectively deployed wealth of the human being that the wealth of subjective *human* sensibility (a musical ear, an eye which is sensitive to the beauty of form, in short, senses which are capable of human satisfaction and which confirm themselves as human faculties) is cultivated or created. For it is not only the five senses, but also the so-called spiritual senses, the practical senses (desiring, loving, etc.), in brief, human sensibility and the human character of the senses, which can only come into being through the existence of *its* object, through humanized nature. The cultivation of the five senses is the work of all previous history. Sense which is subservient to crude needs has only a restricted meaning. For a starving man the human form of food does not exist, but only its abstract character as food. It could just as well exist in the most crude form, and it is impossible to say in what way this feeding-activity would differ from that of animals. The needy man, burdened with cares, has no appreciation of the most beautiful spectacle. The dealer in minerals sees only their commercial value, not their beauty or their particular characteristics; he has no mineralogical sense. Thus, the objectification of the human essence, both theoretically and practically, is necessary in order to *humanize* man's senses, and also to create the *human senses* corresponding to all the wealth of human and natural being.

Just as society at its beginnings finds, through the development of *private property* with its wealth and poverty (both intellectual and material), the materials necessary for this *cultural development*, so the fully constituted society produces man in all the plenitude of his being, the wealthy man endowed with all the senses, as an enduring reality. It is only in a social context that subjectivism and objectivism, spiritualism and materialism, activity and passivity, cease to be antinomies and thus cease to exist as such antinomies. The resolution of the *theoretical* contradictions is possible *only* through practical means, only through the *practical* energy of man. Their resolution is not by any means, therefore, only a problem of knowledge, but is a *real* problem of life which philosophy was unable to solve precisely because it saw there a purely theoretical problem.

It can be seen that the history of *industry* and industry as it *objectively* exists is an *open* book of the *human faculties*, and a human *psychology* which can be sensuously apprehended. This history has not so far been conceived in relation to human *nature*, but only from a superficial utilitarian point of view, since in the condition of alienation it was only possible to conceive real human faculties and *human* species-action in the form of general human existence, as religion, or as history in its abstract, general aspect as politics, art and literature, etc. *Everyday material industry* (which can be conceived as part of that general development; or equally, the general development can be conceived as a specific part of industry since all human activity up to the present has been labour, i.e. industry, self-alienated activity) shows us, in the form of *sensuous useful objects*, in an alienated form, the *essential human faculties* transformed into objects. No psychology for which this book, i.e. the most tangible and accessible part of history, remains closed, can become a *real* science with a genuine content. What is to be thought of a science which stays aloof from this enormous field of human labour, and which does not feel its own inadequacy even though this great wealth of human activity means nothing to it except perhaps what can be expressed in the single phrase— " need," " common need " ?

The *natural sciences* have developed a tremendous activity and have assembled an ever-growing mass of data. But philosophy has remained alien to these sciences just as they have remained alien to philosophy. Their momentary *rapprochement* was only a *fantastic* illusion. There was a desire for union but the power to effect it was lacking. Historiography itself only takes natural science into account incidentally, regarding it as a factor making for enlightenment, for practical utility and for particular great discoveries. But natural science has penetrated all the more *practically* into human life through industry. It has transformed human life and prepared the emancipation of humanity, even though its immediate effect was to accentuate the dehumanization of man. *Industry* is the actual historical relationship of nature, and thus of natural science, to man. If industry is conceived as the *exoteric* manifestation of the essential human *faculties*, the *human* essence of nature and the *natural* essence of man can also be understood. Natural science will then abandon its abstract materialist, or rather idealist, orientation, and will become the basis of a *human* science, just as it has already become—though in an alienated form—the basis of actual human life. One basis for life and another for science is *a priori* a falsehood. Nature, as it develops in human history, in the act of genesis of human society, is the *actual* nature of man; thus nature, as it develops through industry, though in an *alienated* form, is truly *anthropological* nature.

Sense experience (*see* Feuerbach) must be the basis of all science. Science is only genuine science when it proceeds from sense experience, in the two forms of *sense perception* and *sensuous* need; i.e. only when it proceeds from nature. The whole of history is a preparation for " man " to become an object of *sense* perception, and for the development of human needs (the needs of man as such). History itself is a *real* part of *natural history*, of the development of nature into man. Natural science will one day incorporate the science of man, just as the science of man will incorporate natural science; there will be a *single* science.

Man is the direct object of natural science, because directly *perceptible nature* is for man directly human sense experience (an identical expression) in the form of the *other person* who is directly presented to him in a sensuous way. His own sense experience only exists as human sense experience for himself through the *other person*. But *nature* is the direct object of the *science of man*. The first object for man—man himself—is nature, sense experience; and the particular sensuous human faculties, which can only find objective realization in *natural* objects, can only attain self-knowledge in the science of natural being. The element of thought itself, the element of the living manifestation of thought, language, is sensuous in character. The *social* reality of nature and *human* natural science, or the *natural science of man*, are identical expressions.

It will be seen from this how, in place of the *wealth* and *poverty* of political economy, we have the *wealthy* man and the plenitude of *human* need. The wealthy man is at the same time one who *needs* a complex of human manifestations of life, and whose own self-realization exists as an inner necessity, a *need*. Not only the wealth but also the *poverty* of man acquires, in a socialist perspective, a *human* and thus a social meaning. Poverty is the passive bond which leads man to experience a need for the greatest wealth, the *other* person. The sway of the objective entity within me, the sensuous eruption of my life-activity, is the passion which here becomes the *activity* of my being.

A being does not regard himself as independent unless he is his own master, and he is only his own master when he owes his existence to himself. A man who lives by the favour of another considers himself a dependent being. But I live completely by another person's favour when I owe to him not only the continuance of my life but also *its creation*; when he is its *source*. My life has necessarily such a cause outside itself if it is not my own creation. The idea of *creation* is thus one which it is difficult to eliminate from popular consciousness. This consciousness is *unable to conceive* that nature and man exist on their own account, because such an existence contradicts all the tangible facts of practical life.

The idea of the creation of the *earth* has received a severe blow from the science of geogeny, i.e. from the science which portrays the formation and development of the earth as a process of spontaneous generation. *Generatio aequivoca* (spontaneous generation) is the only practical refutation of the theory of creation.

But it is easy indeed to say to the particular individual what Aristotle said: You are engendered by your father and mother, and consequently it is the coitus of two human beings, a human species-act, which has produced the human being. You see, therefore, that even in a physical sense man owes his existence to man. Consequently, it is not enough to keep in view only one of the two aspects, the *infinite* progression, and to ask further: who engendered my father and my grandfather? You must also keep in mind the *circular movement* which is perceptible in that progression, according to which man, in the act of generation reproduces himself; thus *man* always remains the subject. But you will reply: I grant you this circular movement, but you must in turn concede the progression, which leads ever further to the point where I ask; who created the first man and nature as a whole? I can only reply: your question is itself a product of abstraction. Ask yourself how you arrive at that question. Ask yourself whether your question does not arise from a point of view to which I cannot reply because it is a perverted one. Ask yourself whether that progression exists as such for rational thought. If you ask a question about the creation of nature and man you abstract from nature and man. You suppose them *non-existent* and you want me to demonstrate that they *exist*. I reply: give up your abstraction and at the same time you abandon your question. Or else, if you want to maintain your abstraction, be consistent, and if you think of man and nature as non-existent, [XI] think of yourself too as non-existent, for you are also man and nature. Do not think, do not ask me any questions, for as soon as you think and ask questions your abstraction from the existence of nature and man becomes meaningless. Or are you such an egoist that you conceive everything as non-existent and yet want to exist yourself?

You may reply: I do not want to conceive the nothingness of nature, etc.; I only ask you about the act of its creation, just as I ask the anatomist about the formation of bones, etc.

Since, however, for socialist man, the *whole of what is called world history* is nothing but the creation of man by human labour, and the emergence of nature for man, he, therefore, has the evident and irrefutable proof of his *self-creation*, of his own *origins*. Once the essence of man and of nature, man as a natural being and nature as a human reality, has become evident in practical life, in sense experience, the quest for an *alien* being, a being above man and nature (a quest which is an avowal of the unreality of man and nature) becomes impossible in practice. *Atheism*, as a denial of this unreality, is no longer meaningful, for atheism is a *negation of God* and seeks to assert by this negation the *existence of man*. Socialism no longer requires such a roundabout method; it begins from the *theoretical* and *practical sense perception* of man and nature as essential beings. It is positive human *self-consciousness*, no longer a self-consciousness attained through the negation of religion; just as the *real life* of man is positive and no longer attained through the negation of private property, through *communism*. Communism is the phase of negation of the negation and is, consequently, for the next stage of historical development, a real and necessary factor in the emancipation and rehabilitation of man. Communism is the necessary form and the dynamic principle of the immediate future, but communism is not itself the goal of human development—the form of human society.

NEEDS, PRODUCTION, AND DIVISION OF LABOUR

[XIV] (7) WE have seen the importance which must be attributed, in a socialist perspective, to the *wealth* of human needs, and consequently also to a *new mode of production* and to a new *object* of production. A new manifestation of *human* powers and a new enrichment of the human being. Within the system of private property it has the opposite meaning. Every man speculates upon creating a *new* need in another in order to force him to a new sacrifice, to place him in a new dependence, and to entice him into a new kind of pleasure and thereby into economic ruin. Everyone tries to establish over others an alien power in order to find there the satisfaction of his own egoistic need. With the increasing mass of objects, therefore, the realm of alien entities to which man is subjected also increases. Every new product is a new *potentiality* of mutual deceit and robbery. Man becomes increasingly poor as a man; he has increasing need of *money* in order to take possession of the hostile being. The power of his *money* diminishes directly with the growth of the quantity of production, i.e. his need increases with the increasing *power* of money. The need for money is, therefore, the real need created by the modern economic system, and the only need which it creates. The *quantity* of money becomes increasingly its only important quality. Just as it reduces every entity to an abstraction, so it reduces itself in its own development to a *quantitative* entity. Excess and immoderation become its true standard. This is shown subjectively, partly in the fact that the expansion of production and of needs becomes an *ingenious* and always *calculating* subservience to inhuman, depraved, unnatural and *imaginary* appetites. Private property does not know how to change crude need into *human* need; its *idealism* is *fantasy*, *caprice* and *fancy*.

No eunuch flatters his tyrant more shamefully or seeks by more infamous means to stimulate his jaded appetite, in order to gain some favour, than does the eunuch of industry, the entrepreneur, in order to acquire a few silver coins or to charm the gold from the purse of his dearly beloved neighbour. (Every product is a bait by means of which the individual tries to entice the essence of the other person, his money. Every real or potential need is a weakness which will draw the bird into the lime. Universal exploitation of human communal life. Just as every imperfection of man is a bond with heaven, a point from which his heart is accessible to the priest, so every want is an opportunity for approaching one's neighbour, in simulated friendship, and saying, " Dear friend, I will give you what you need, but you know the *conditio sine qua non*. You know what ink you must use in signing yourself over to me. I shall swindle you while providing your enjoyment.") The entrepreneur accedes to the most depraved fancies of his neighbour, plays the role of pander between him and his needs, awakens unhealthy appetites in him, and watches for every weakness so that later on he may claim the remuneration for this labour of love.

This alienation is shown in part by the fact that the refinement of needs and of the means to satisfy them produces as its counterpart a bestial savagery, a complete, primitive and abstract simplicity of needs; or rather, that it simply reproduces itself in its opposite sense. For the worker even the need for fresh air ceases to be a need. Man returns to the cave dwelling again, but it is now poisoned by the pestilential breath of civilization. The worker has only a *precarious* right to inhabit it, for it has become an alien dwelling which may suddenly not be available, or from which he may be evicted if he [XV] does not pay the rent. He has to *pay* for this mortuary. The dwelling full of light which Aeschylus' Prometheus indicates as one of the great gifts by which he has changed savages into men, ceases to exist for the worker. Light, air, and the simplest *animal* cleanliness cease to be human needs. *Filth*, this corruption and putrefaction which runs in the *sewers* of civilization (this is to be taken literally) becomes the *element in which man lives*. Total and *unnatural* neglect, putrefied nature, becomes the *element in which he lives*. None of his senses exist any longer, either in a human form, or even in a non-human, animal form. The crudest *methods* (and *instruments*) of human labour reappear; thus the *treadmill* of the Roman slaves has become the mode of production and mode of existence of many English workers. It is not enough that man should lose his human needs; even animal needs disappear. The Irish no longer have any need but that of *eating—eating potatoes*, and then only the worst kind, *mildewed potatoes*. But France and England already possess in every industrial town a *little* Ireland. Savages and animals have at least the need for hunting, exercise and companionship. But the simplification of machinery and of work is used to make workers out of those who are just growing up, who are still immature, *children*, while the worker himself has become a child deprived of all care. Machinery is adapted to the weakness of the human being, in order to turn the weak human being into a machine.

The fact that the growth of needs and of the means to satisfy them results in a lack of needs and of means is demonstrated in several ways by the economist (and by the capitalist; in fact, it is always empirical businessmen we refer to when we speak of economists, who are their *scientific* self-revelation and existence). First, by reducing the needs of the worker to the miserable necessities required for the maintenance of his physical existence, and by reducing his activity to the most abstract mechanical movements, the economist asserts that man has no needs, for activity or enjoyment, beyond that; and yet he declares that this kind of life is a *human* way of life. Secondly, by reckoning as the general standard of life (general because it is applicable to the mass of men) the *most impoverished* life conceivable, he turns the worker into a being who has neither senses nor needs, just as he turns his activity into a pure abstraction from all activity.   Thus all working-class *luxury* seems to him blameworthy, and everything which goes beyond the most abstract need (whether it be a passive enjoyment or a manifestation of personal activity) is regarded as a *luxury*. Political economy, the science of *wealth*, is, therefore, at the same time, the science of renunciation, of privation and of saving, which actually succeeds in depriving man of fresh *air* and of physical *activity*.   This science of a marvellous in-dustry is at the same time the science of *asceticism*.   Its true ideal is the *ascetic* but *usurious* miser and the *ascetic* but *productive* slave.   Its moral ideal is the *worker* who takes a part of his wages to the savings bank.   It has even found a servile art to embody this favourite idea, which has been produced in a sentimental manner on the stage.   Thus, despite its worldly and pleasure-seeking appearance, it is a truly moral science, and the most moral of all sciences.   Its principal thesis is the renunciation of life and of human needs.   The less you eat, drink, buy books, go to the theatre or to balls, or to the public house, and the less you think, love, theorize, sing, paint, fence, etc. the more you will be able to save and the *greater* will become your treasure which neither moth nor rust will corrupt—your *capital*.   The less you *are*, the less you express your life, the more you *have*, the greater is your *alienated* life and the greater is the saving of your alienated being. Everything [XVI] which the economist takes from you in the way of life and humanity, he restores to you in the form of *money* and *wealth*.   And everything which you are unable to do, your money can do for you; it can eat, drink, go to the ball and to the theatre. It can acquire art, learning, historical treasures, political power; and it can travel.   It *can* appropriate all these things for you, can purchase everything; it is the true *opulence*.   But although it can do all this, it only *desires* to create itself, and to buy itself, for everything else is subservient to it. When one owns the master, one also owns the servant, and one has no need of the master's servant. Thus all passions and activities must be submerged in *avarice*. The worker must have just what is necessary for him to want to live, and he must want to live only in order to have this.

It is true that some controversy has arisen in the field of political economy. Some economists (Lauderdale, Malthus, *et al.*) advocate luxury and condemn saving, while others (Ricardo, Say, *et al.*) advocate saving and condemn luxury. But the former admit that they desire luxury in order to create *work*, i.e. absolute saving, while the latter admit that they advocate saving in order to create *wealth*, i.e. luxury. The former have the *romantic* notion that avarice alone should not determine the consumption of the rich, and they contradict their own laws when they represent *prodigality* as being a direct means of enrichment; their opponents then demonstrate in detail and with great earnestness that prodigality diminishes rather than augments my *possessions*. The second group are hypocritical in not admitting that it is caprice and fancy which determine production. They forget the " refined needs," and that without consumption there would be no production. They forget that through competition production must become ever more universal and luxurious, that it is use which determines the value of a thing, and that use is determined by fashion. They want production to be limited to " useful things," but they forget that the production of too many useful things results in too many *useless* people. Both sides forget that prodigality and thrift, luxury and abstinence, wealth and poverty are equivalent.

You must not only be abstemious in the satisfaction of your direct senses, such as eating, etc., but also in your participation in general interests, your sympathy, trust, etc. if you wish to be economical and to avoid being ruined by illusions.

Everything which you own must be made *venal*, i.e. useful. Suppose I ask the economist: am I acting in accordance with economic laws if I earn money by the sale of my body, by prostituting it to another person's lust (in France, the factory workers call the prostitution of their wives and daughters the *n*th hour of work, which is literally true); or if I sell my friends to the Moroccans (and the direct sale of men occurs in all civilized countries in the form of the trade in conscripts)? He will reply: you are not acting contrary to my laws, but you must take into account what Cousin Morality and Cousin Religion have to say. My *economic* morality and religion have no objection to make, but . . . But then whom should we believe, the economist or the moralist? The morality of political economy is *gain*, work, thrift and sobriety—yet political economy promises to satisfy my needs. The political economy of morality is the riches of a good conscience, of virtue, etc., but how can I be virtuous if I am not alive and how can I have a good conscience if I am not aware of anything? The nature of alienation implies that each sphere applies a different and contradictory norm, that morality does not apply the same norm as political economy, etc., because each of them is a particular alienation of man; [XVII] each is concentrated upon a specific area of alienated activity and is itself alienated from the other.

Thus M. Michel Chevalier reproaches Ricardo with leaving morals out of account. But Ricardo lets political economy speak its own language; he is not to blame if this language is not that of morals. M. Chevalier ignores political economy in so far as he concerns himself with morals, but he really and necessarily ignores morals when he is concerned with political economy; for the bearing of political economy upon morals is either arbitrary and accidental and thus lacking any scientific basis or character, is a mere *sham*, or else it is *essential* and can then only be a relation between economic laws and morals. If there is no such relation, can Ricardo be held responsible? More-over, the antithesis between morals and political economy is itself only *apparent*; there is an antithesis and equally no antithesis. Political economy expresses, *in its own fashion*, the moral laws.

The absence of needs, as the principle of political economy, is shown in the most *striking* way in its *theory of population*. There are *too many* men. The very existence of man is a pure luxury, and if the worker is " *moral* " he will be *economical* in procreation. (Mill proposes that public commendation should be given to those who show themselves abstemious in sexual relations, and public condemnation to those who sin against the sterility of marriage. Is this not the moral doctrine of asceticism?) The production of men appears as a public misfortune.

The significance which production has in relation to the wealthy is *revealed* in the significance which it has for the poor. At the top its manifestation is always refined, con-cealed, ambiguous, an appearance; at the bottom it is rough, straightforward, candid, a reality. The *crude* need of the worker is a much greater source of profit than the *refined* need of the wealthy. The cellar dwellings in London bring their landlords more than do the palaces; i.e. they constitute *greater wealth* so far as the landlord is concerned and thus, in economic terms, greater *social* wealth.

Just as industry speculates upon the refinement of needs so also it speculates upon their *crudeness*, and upon their artificially produced crudeness whose spirit, therefore, is *self-stupefaction*, the *illusory* satisfaction of needs, a civilization *within* the crude barbarism of need. The English gin-shops are, therefore, symbolic representations of private property. Their *luxury* reveals the real relation of industrial luxury and wealth to man. They are, therefore, rightly the only Sunday enjoyment of the people, treated mildly at least by the English police.

We have already seen how the economist establishes the

unity of labour and capital in various ways: (1) capital is *accumulated* labour; (2) the purpose of capital within production—partly the reproduction of capital with profit, partly capital as raw material (material of labour), partly capital as itself a *working instrument* (the machine is fixed capital which is identical with labour)—is *productive work*; (3) the worker is capital; (4) wages form part of the costs of capital; (5) for the worker, labour is the reproduction of his life-capital; (6) for the capitalist, labour is a factor in the activity of his capital.

Finally (7) the economist postulates the original unity of capital and labour as the unity of capitalist and worker. This is the original paradisaical condition. How these two factors, [XIX] as two persons, spring at each other's throats is for the economist a *ortuitous* occurrence, which, therefore, requires only to be explained by external circumstances (*see* Mill).

The nations which are still dazzled by the sensuous glitter of precious metals and who thus remain fetishists of metallic money are not yet fully developed money nations. Contrast between France and England. The extent to which the solution of a theoretical problem is a task of practice, and is accomplished through practice, and the extent to which correct practice is the condition of a true and positive theory is shown, for example, in the case of *fetishism*. The sense perception of a fetishist differs from that of a Greek because his sensuous existence is different. The abstract hostility between sense and spirit is inevitable so long as the human sense for nature, or the human meaning of nature, and consequently the *natural* sense of *man*, has not been produced through man's own labour.

Equality is nothing but the German "Ich=Ich" translated into the French, i.e. political, form. Equality as the *basis* of communism is a *political* foundation; and it is the same as when the German bases communism upon the fact that he conceives man as *universal self-consciousness*. Of course, the transcendence of alienation always proceeds from the form of alienation which is the *dominant* power; in Germany, *self-consciousness*; in France, *equality*, because politics; in England, the real, material, self-sufficient, *practical* need. Proudhon should be appreciated and criticized from this point of view.

If we now characterize *communism* itself (for as negation of the negation, as the appropriation of human existence which mediates itself with itself through the negation of private property, it is not the *true*, self-originating position, but rather one which begins from private property) . . . [1] the alienation of human life remains and a much greater alienation remains the more one is conscious of it as such) can only be accomplished by the establishment of communism. In order to supersede the *idea* of private property communist *ideas* are sufficient, but *genuine* communist activity is necessary in order to supersede *real* private property. History will produce it, and the development which we already recognize in thought as self-transcending will in reality involve a severe and protracted process. We must consider it an advance, however, that we have previously acquired an awareness of the limited nature and the goal of the historical development and can see beyond it.

When communist *artisans* form associations, teaching and propaganda are their first aims. But their association itself creates a new need—the need for society—and what appeared to be a means has become an end. The most striking results of this practical development are to be seen when French socialist workers meet together. Smoking, eating and drinking are no longer simply means of bringing people together. Society, association, entertainment which also has society as its aim, is sufficient for them; the brotherhood of man is no empty phrase but a reality, and the nobility of man shines forth upon us from their toil-worn bodies.

---

[1] A part of the page is torn away here, and there follow fragments of six lines which are insufficient to reconstruct the passage. [*Editor's note.*]

[XX] When political economy asserts that supply and demand always balance each other, it forgets at once its own contention (the theory of population) that the supply of *men* always exceeds the demand, and consequently, that the disproportion between supply and demand is most strikingly expressed in the essential end of production—the existence of man.

The extent to which money, which has the appearance of a means, is the real power and the unique *end*, and in general the extent to which *the* means which gives me being and possession of the alien objective being, is an *end in itself*, can be seen from the fact that landed property, where land is the source of life, and *horse* and *sword*, where these are the *real means of life*, are also recognized as the real political powers. In the middle ages an estate becomes emancipated when it has the right to carry the sword.   Among nomadic peoples it is the *horse* which makes me a free man and a member of the community.

We said above that man is regressing to the *cave dwelling*, but in an alienated, malignant form.   The savage in his cave (a natural element which is freely offered for his use and protection) does not feel himself a stranger; on the contrary he feels as much at home as a *fish* in water.   But the cellar dwelling of the poor man is a hostile dwelling, " an alien, constricting power which only surrenders itself to him in exchange for blood and sweat."   He cannot regard it as his home, as a place where he might at last say, " here I am at home."   Instead, he finds himself in *another person's* house, the house of a *stranger* who lies in wait for him every day and evicts him if he does not pay the rent.   He is also aware of the contrast between his own dwelling and a human dwelling such as exists in *that other world*, the heaven of wealth.

Alienation is apparent not only in the fact that *my* means of life belong to *someone else*, that *my* desires are the unattainable possession of *someone else*, but that everything is *something different* from itself, that my activity is *something else*, and finally (and this is also the case for the capitalist) that *an inhuman power* rules over everything. There is a kind of wealth which is inactive, prodigal and devoted to pleasure, the beneficiary of which *behaves* as an *ephemeral*, aimlessly active individual who regards the slave labour of others, human *blood and sweat*, as the prey of his cupidity, and who sees mankind and himself as a sacrificial and superfluous being. Thus he acquires a contempt for mankind, expressed in the form of arrogance and the squandering of resources which would support a hundred human lives, and also in the form of the infamous illusion that his unbridled extravagance and endless unproductive consumption is a condition for the *labour* and *subsistence* of others. He regards the realization of the *essential powers* of man only as the realization of his own disorderly life, his whims and his capricious, bizarre ideas. Such wealth, however, which sees wealth merely as a means, as something to be consumed, and which is, therefore, both master and slave, generous and mean, capricious, presumptuous, conceited, refined, cultured and witty, has not yet discovered *wealth* as a wholly *alien power* but sees in it its own power and enjoyment rather than wealth . . . final aim.[1]

. . . [XXI] and the glittering illusion about the nature of wealth produced by its dazzling sensuous appearance, is confronted by the *hard-working, sober, economical, prosaic* industrialist who is enlightened about the nature of wealth and who, while increasing the scope of the other's self-indulgence and flattering him by his products (for his products are just so many base compliments to the spendthrift's appetites) knows how to appropriate to himself, in the only *useful* way, the other's declining power. Although, therefore, industrial wealth appears at first to be the product of prodigal, fantastic wealth, it nevertheless dispossesses the

---

[1] The bottom of the page is torn and several lines of the text are missing. [*Editor's note.*]

latter in an active way by its own development. The fall in the *rate of interest* is a necessary consequence of industrial development. Thus the resources of the spendthrift rentier dwindle *in proportion to* the increase in the means and occasions of enjoyment. He is obliged either to consume his capital and thus ruin himself, or to become an industrial capitalist himself . . . On the other hand, there is a constant increase in the *rent of land* in the course of industrial development, but as we have already seen there must come a time when landed property, like every other form of property, falls into the category of capital which reproduces itself through profit—and this is a result of the same industrial development. Thus the spendthrift landowner must either squander his capital and ruin himself, or become the tenant farmer of his own estate—an agricultural industrialist.

The decline in the rate of interest (which Proudhon regards as the abolition of capital and as a tendency towards the socialization of capital) is thus rather a direct symptom of the complete victory of working capital over spendthrift wealth, i.e. the transformation of all private property into industrial capital. It is the complete victory of private property over all its *apparently* human qualities, and the total subjection of the property owner to the essence of private property—*labour*. Of course, the industrial capitalist also has his pleasures. He does not by any means return to an unnatural simplicity in his needs, but his enjoyment is only a secondary matter; it is recreation subordinated to production and thus a *calculated, economic* enjoyment, for he charges his pleasures as an expense of capital and what he squanders must not be more than can be replaced with profit by the reproduction of capital. Thus enjoyment is subordinated to capital and the pleasure-loving individual is subordinated to the capital-accumulating individual, whereas formerly the contrary was the case. The decline in the rate of interest is, therefore, only a symptom of the abolition of capital in so far as it is a symptom of its increasing domination and increasing alienation which hastens its own abolition. In general, this is the only way in which that which exists affirms its opposite.

The dispute between economists over luxury and saving is, therefore, only a dispute between the political economy which has become clearly aware of the nature of wealth and that political economy which is still burdened with romantic, anti-industrial memories. Neither side, however, knows how to express the subject of the dispute in simple terms, or is able, therefore, to settle the issue.

Further, the *rent of land*, *qua* rent of land, has been abolished; for against the argument of the Physiocrats that the landowner is the only genuine producer, modern political economy demonstrates rather that the landowner as such is the only completely unproductive rentier. Agriculture is the affair of the capitalist, who employs his capital in it when he can expect a normal rate of profit. The assertion of the Physiocrats that landed property as the only productive property should alone pay taxes, and consequently should alone sanction them and participate in state affairs, is transformed into the contrary conviction that the taxes upon the rent of land are the only taxes upon an unproductive revenue and thus the only ones which are not detrimental to the national output. It is evident that from this point of view no political privileges for the landowners follow from their situation as the principal taxpayers.

Everything which Proudhon conceives as a movement of labour against capital is only the movement of labour in the form of capital, of *industrial capital* against that which is not consumed *as* capital, i.e. industrially. And this movement goes upon its triumphant way, the way of the victory of industrial capital. It will be seen that only when labour is conceived as the essence of private property can the real characteristics of the economic movement itself be analysed.

Society, as it appears to the economist, is *civil* society, in which each individual is a totality of needs and only exists for another person, as the other exists for him, in so far as each becomes a means for the other. The economist (like politics in its *rights of man*) reduces everything to man, i.e. to the individual, whom he deprives of all characteristics in order to classify him as a capitalist or a worker.

The *division of labour* is the economic expression of the *social character of labour* within alienation. Or, since *labour* is only an expression of human activity within alienation, of life activity as alienation of life, the *division of labour* is nothing but the *alienated* establishment of human activity as a *real species-activity* or *the activity of man as a species-being*.

The economists are very confused and self-contradictory about the nature of the *division of labour* (which of course has to be regarded as a principal motive force in the production of wealth once labour is recognized as the *essence of private property*), i.e. about the *alienated form of human activity as species-activity*.

Adam Smith: " The division of labour . . . is not originally the effect of any human wisdom. . . . It is the necessary, though very slow and gradual consequence of the propensity to truck, barter and exchange one thing for another. [Whether this propensity be one of those original principles of human nature . . .] or whether, as seems more probable, it be the necessary consequence of the faculties of reason and of speech [it belongs not to our present subject to inquire]. It is common to all men, and to be found in no other race of animals . . . [In almost every other race of animals the individual] when it is grown up to maturity is entirely independent. . . . But man has almost constant occasion for the help of his brethren, and it is in vain for him to expect it from their benevolence only. He will be more likely to prevail if he can interest their self-love in his favour, and show them that it is for their own advantage to do for him what he requires of them. . . . We address ourselves

not to their humanity but to their self-love, and never talk
to them of our own necessities but of their advantages." [1]

" As it is by treaty, by barter, and by purchase that we
obtain from one another the greater part of those mutual
good offices that we stand in need of, so it is this same trucking
disposition which originally gives occasion to the division of
labour. In a tribe of hunters or shepherds a particular
person makes bows and arrows, for example, with more
readiness and dexterity than any other. He frequently exchanges them for cattle or for venison with his companions;
and he finds at last that he can in this manner get more cattle
and venison than if he himself went to the field to catch them.
From a regard to his own interest, therefore, the making of
bows and arrows grows to be his chief business. . . . " [2]

" The difference of natural talents in different men . . .
is not . . . so much the cause as the effect of the division
of labour. . . . Without the disposition to truck, barter
and exchange, every man must have procured to himself
every necessary and conveniency of life which he wanted.
All must have had . . . the same work to do, and there
could have been no such difference of employment as could
alone give occasion to any great difference of talents." [3]

" As it is this disposition which forms that difference of
talents . . . among men, so it is this same disposition which
renders that difference useful. Many tribes of animals . . .
of the same species derive from nature a much more re-
markable distinction of genius than what, antecedent to
custom and education, appears to take place among men.
By nature a philosopher is not in genius and in disposition
half so different from a street-porter, as a mastiff is from a
greyhound, or a greyhound from a spaniel, or this last from
a shepherd's dog. Those different tribes of animals, however, though all of the same species, are of scarce any use to

---

[1] ADAM SMITH, op. cit., I, pp. 12–13. I have indicated the parts of this
quotation which Marx paraphrased by square brackets. [*Editor's note.*]

[2] Ibid., pp. 13–14.   [3] Ibid., p. 14.

one another.   The strength of the mastiff [XXXVI] is not, in the least, supported either by the swiftness of the grey-hound, or . . . The effects of those different geniuses and talents, for want of the power or disposition to barter and exchange, cannot be brought into a common stock, and do not in the least contribute to the better accommodation and conveniency of the species.   Each animal is still obliged to support and defend itself, separately and independently, and derives no sort of advantage from that variety of talents with which nature has distinguished its fellows.   Among men, on the contrary, the most dissimilar geniuses are of use to one another; the different produces of their respective talents, by the general disposition to truck, barter and exchange, being brought, as it were, into a common stock, where every man may purchase whatever part of the produce of other men's talents he has occasion for." [1]

" As it is the power of exchanging that gives occasion to the division of labour, so the extent of this division must always be limited by the extent of that power, or, in other words, by the extent of the market.   When the market is very small, no person can have any encouragement to dedi-cate himself entirely to one employment, for want of the power to exchange all that surplus part of the produce of his own labour, which is over and above his own consumption, for such parts of the produce of other men's labour as he has occasion for." [2]

In an advanced state of society: " Every man thus lives by exchanging, or becomes in some measure a merchant, and the society itself grows to be what is properly a commercial society." [3]   (See Destutt de Tracy: [4] " Society is a series of reciprocal exchanges; commerce contains the whole essence of society.")   The accumulation of capital increases with the division of labour and vice-versa.—Thus far Adam Smith.

---

[1] SMITH, op cit., I, pp. 14–15.   [2] Ibid., p. 15.   [3] Ibid., p. 20.
[4] DESTUTT DE TRACEY, Eléments d'idéologie.   Traité de la volonté et de ses effets.   2 ème édition.   Paris, 1818, pp. 131, 143.

" . . . if every family . . . produced all that it consumed society could keep going although no exchange of any kind took place . . . in our advanced state of society, exchange, though *not fundamental*, is indispensable." [1] " The division of labour is a skilful employment of man's powers; it increases society's production—its power and its pleasures—but it diminishes the ability of every person taken individually." [2] Production cannot take place without exchange.—Thus J. B. Say.

" The powers inherent in man are his intelligence and his physical capacity for work. Those which arise from the condition of society consist of the capacity to divide and to distribute among different people the tasks necessary for procuring the means of subsistence [and of increasing their well-being]; and the capacity to exchange the services and products which constitute these means. . . . [The motive which impels a man to give his services to another is self-interest; he requires a return for the services rendered. The right of exclusive private property is indispensable to the establishment of exchange among men. . . . Exchange and division of labour mutually condition each other.] " [3] —Thus Skarbek.

Mill presents developed exchange—*trade*—as a *consequence* of the *division of labour*: " . . . the agency of man can be traced to very simple elements. He can, in fact, do nothing more than produce motion. He can move things towards one another, and he can separate them from one another [XXXVII]: the properties of matter perform all the rest. . . . In the employment of labour and machinery, it is often found that the effects can be increased by skilful

---

[1] JEAN-BAPTISTE SAY, op. cit., I, p. 300. Emphasis added by Marx. [*Editor's note.*]

[2] Ibid., pp. 76–7.

[3] F. SKARBEK, *Théorie des richesses sociales, suivie d'une bibliographie de l'économie politique.* Paris 1829. Tomes I–II; I, p. 25. The final section enclosed in square brackets is a paraphase of statements taken from various chapters of Skarbek's book. [*Editor's note.*]

distribution, by separating all those operations which have any tendency to impede one another, by bringing together all those operations which can be made in any way to aid one another. As men in general cannot perform many different operations with the same quickness and dexterity with which they can by practice learn to perform a few, it is always an advantage to limit as much as possible the number of operations imposed upon each. For dividing labour, and distributing the powers of men and machinery, to the greatest advantage, it is in most cases necessary to operate upon a large scale; in other words, to produce the commodities in great masses. It is this advantage which gives existence to the great manufactories; a few of which, placed in the most convenient situations, sometimes supply not one country, but many countries, with as much as they desire of the commodity produced." [1]—Thus Mill.

The whole of modern political economy is agreed, however, upon the fact that division of labour and abundance of production, division of labour and accumulation of capital, are mutually determining; and also that liberated and autonomous private property alone can produce the most effective and extensive division of labour.

Adam Smith's argument may be summarized as follows: The division of labour confers upon labour an unlimited capacity to produce. It arises from the *propensity to exchange and barter*, a specifically human propensity which is probably not fortuitous but determined by the use of reason and speech. The motive of those who engage in exchange is not humanity but *egoism*. The diversity of human talents is more the effect than the cause of the division of labour, i.e. of exchange. Furthermore, it is only the latter which makes this diversity useful. The particular qualities of the different tribes within an animal species are by nature more

[1] JAMES MILL, *Elements of Political Economy*, London, 1821, pp. 5–9. Marx quotes from the French translation by J. T. Parisot (Paris 1823). [*Editor's note*.]

pronounced than the differences between the aptitudes and activities of human beings. But since animals are not able to exchange, the diversity of qualities in animals of the same species but of different tribes is of no benefit to any individual animal. Animals are unable to combine the various qualities of their species, or to contribute to the *common* advantage and comfort of the species. It is otherwise with *men*, whose most diverse talents and forms of activity are useful to each other, *because* they can bring their *different* products together in a common stock, from which each man can buy. As the division of labour arises from the propensity to *exchange*, so it develops and is limited by the *extent of exchange*, by the *extent of the market*. In developed conditions every man is a *merchant* and society is a *commercial association*. Say regards *exchange* as fortuitous and not fundamental. Society could exist without it. It becomes indispensable in an advanced state of society. Yet *production* cannot take place *without it*. The division of labour is a *convenient* and *useful* means, a skilful deployment of human powers for social wealth, but it diminishes *the capacity of each person* taken *individually*. The last remark is an advance on the part of Say.

Skarbek distinguishes the *individual innate* powers of man, intelligence and physical capacity for work, from the powers *derived* from society—*exchange and division of labour* which mutually determine each other. But the necessary precondition of exchange is private property. Skarbek here expresses objectively what Smith, Say, Ricardo, *et al.* say when they designate *egoism* and *self-interest* as the basis of exchange, and *commercial haggling* as the *essential* and *adequate* form of exchange.

Mill represents *trade* as the consequence of the *division of labour*. For him, human activity is reduced to mechanical motion. The division of labour and the use of machinery promote abundance of production. Each individual must be given the smallest possible range of operations. The division of labour and the use of machinery, for their part, require the mass production of wealth, i.e. of products. This is the reason for large-scale manufacture.

[XXXVIII] The consideration of *division of labour* and *exchange* is of the greatest interest, since they are the *perceptible, alienated* expression of human *activity* and *capacities* as the activity and capacities *proper to a species*.

To state that *private property* is the basis of the *division of labour* and *exchange* is simply to assert that *labour* is the essence of private property; an assertion which the economist cannot prove and which we wish to prove for him. It is precisely in the fact that the *division of labour* and *exchange* are manifestations of private property that we find the proof, first that *human* life needed *private property* for its realization, and secondly, that it now requires the supersession of private property.

The *division of labour* and *exchange* are the two phenomena which lead the economist to vaunt the social character of his science, while in the same breath he unconsciously expresses the contradictory nature of his science—the establishment of society through unsocial, particular interests.

The factors we have to consider are as follows: the *propensity to exchange*—whose basis is egoism—is regarded as the cause or the reciprocal effect of the division of labour. Say considers exchange as being not *fundamental* to the nature of society. Wealth and production are explained by the division of labour and exchange. The impoverishment and denaturing of individual activity through the division of labour are admitted. Exchange and division of labour are recognized as the sources of the *great diversity of human talents*, a diversity which in turn becomes useful as a result of exchange. Skarbek distinguishes two parts in man's productive powers: (1) those which are individual and innate, his intelligence and his specific aptitudes or abilities; (2) those which are *derived* not from the real individual, but from society—the division of labour and exchange. Further, the division of labour is limited by the *market*. Human labour is simple *mechanical motion*; the major part is done by the material properties of the objects. The smallest possible number of operations must be allocated to each individual. Fission of labour and concentration of capital; the nullity of individual production and the mass production of wealth. Meaning of free private property in the division of labour.

MONEY

[XLI] If man's *feelings*, passions, etc. are not merely an-thropological characteristics in the narrower sense, but are true *ontological* affirmations of being (nature), and if they are only really affirmed in so far as their *object* exists as an object of sense, then it is evident—

1. that their mode of affirmation is not one and un-changing, but rather that the diverse modes of affirmation constitute the distinctive character of their existence, of their life. The manner in which the object exists for them is the distinctive mode of their *gratification*;

2. where the sensuous affirmation is a direct annulment of the object in its independent form (as in drinking, eating, working up of the object, etc.) this is the affirmation of the object;

3. in so far as man, and hence also his feelings, etc. are *human*, the affirmation of the object by another person is also his own gratification;

4. only through developed industry, i.e. through the mediation of private property, does the ontological essence of human passions, in its totality and its humanity, come into being; the science of man itself is a product of man's self-formation through practical activity;

5. the meaning of private property—released from its alienation—is the *existence of essential objects* for man, as objects of enjoyment and activity.

Money, since it has the *property* of purchasing everything, of appropriating objects to itself, is, therefore, the *object par excellence*. The universal character of this *property* cor-responds to the omnipotence of money, which is regarded as an omnipotent being . . . money is the *pander* between

need and object, between human life and the means of subsistence.   But *that which* mediates *my* life mediates also the
existence of other men for me.   It is for me the *other* person.

> " What, man! confound it, hands and feet
> And head and backside, all are yours!
> And what we take while life is sweet,
> Is that to be declared not ours?
>   Six stallions, say, I can afford,
> Is not their strength my property?
> I tear along, a sporting lord,
> As if their legs belonged to me."
>
> (Goethe, *Faust*—Mephistopheles) [1]

Shakespeare in *Timon of Athens*—

> " Gold? yellow, glittering, precious gold?   No, gods,
> I am no idle votarist: roots, you clear heavens!
> Thus much of this will make black, white; foul, fair;
> Wrong, right; base, noble; old, young; coward, valiant.
> . . . Why this
> Will lug your priests and servants from your sides;
> Pluck stout men's pillows from below their heads:
> This yellow slave
> Will knit and break religions; bless th'accurst;
> Make the hoar leprosy ador'd; place thieves,
> And give them title, knee, and approbation,
> With senators on the bench: this is it
> That makes the wappen'd widow wed again;
> She whom the spital-house and ulcerous sores
> Would cast the gorge at, this embalms and spices
> To th'April day again.   Come, damned earth,
> Thou common whore of mankind, that putt'st odds
> Among the rout of nations, I will make thee
> Do thy right nature." [2]

And later on—

> " O thou sweet king-killer, and dear divorce
> 'Twixt natural son and sire!   Thou bright defiler
> Of Hymen's purest bed!   Thou valiant Mars!
> Thou ever young, fresh, loved and delicate wooer,
> Whose blush doth thaw the consecrated snow

---

[1] GOETHE, *Faust*.   Part I, Scene 4.   This passage is taken from the translation by Philip Wayne; Penguin Books, 1949.   [*Editor's note.*]

[2] SHAKESPEARE, *Timon of Athens*.   Act IV, Scene 3.   Marx quotes from
the Schlegel-Tieck translation.   [*Editor's note.*]

That lies on Dian's lap! thou visible god,
That solder'st close impossibilities,
And mak'st them kiss! that speak'st with every tongue,
[XLII] To every purpose! O thou touch of hearts!
Think, thy slave man rebels; and by thy virtue
Set them into confounding odds, that beasts
May have the world in empire! " [1]

Shakespeare portrays admirably the nature of *money*. To understand him, let us begin by expounding the passage from Goethe.

That which exists for me through the medium of *money*, that which I can pay for (i.e. which money can buy), that *I am*, the possessor of the money. My own power is as great as the power of money. The properties of money are my own (the possessor's) properties and faculties. What I *am* and *can do* is, therefore, not at all determined by my individuality. I *am* ugly, but I can buy the most beautiful woman for myself. Consequently, I am not *ugly*, for the effect of ugliness, its power to repel, is annulled by money. As an individual I am *lame*, but money provides me with twenty-four legs. Therefore, I am not lame. I am a detestable, dishonourable, unscrupulous and stupid man, but money is honoured and so also is its possessor. Money is the highest good, and so its possessor is good. Besides, money saves me the trouble of being dishonest; therefore, I am presumed honest. I am *stupid*, but since money is *the real mind* of all things, how should its possessor be stupid? Moreover, he can buy talented people for himself, and is not he who has power over the talented more talented than they? I who can have, through the power of money, *everything* for which the human heart longs, do I not possess all human abilities? Does not my money, therefore, transform all my incapacities into their opposites.

If *money* is the bond which binds me to *human* life, and society to me, and which links me with nature and man, is it not the bond of all *bonds*? Is it not, therefore, also the

[1] Loc. cit.

universal agent of separation? It is the real means of both *separation* and *union*, the galvano-*chemical* power of society.

Shakespeare emphasizes particularly two properties of money: (1) it is the visible deity, the transformation of all human and natural qualities into their opposites, the universal confusion and inversion of things; it brings incompatibles into fraternity; (2) it is the universal whore, the universal pander between men and nations.

The power to confuse and invert all human and natural qualities, to bring about fraternization of incompatibles, the *divine* power of money, resides in its *character* as the alienated and self-alienating species-life of man. It is the alienated *power* of *humanity*.

What I as a *man* am unable to do, and thus what all my individual faculties are unable to do, is made possible for me by *money*. Money, therefore, turns each of these faculties into something which it is not, into its *opposite*.

If I long for a meal, or wish to take the mail coach because I am not strong enough to go on foot, money provides the meal and the mail coach; i.e. it transforms my desires from representations into *realities*, from imaginary being into *real being*. In mediating thus money is a *genuinely creative* power.

Demand also exists for the individual who has no money, but his demand is a mere creature of the imagination which has no effect, no existence for me, for a third party, for . . .,[1] (XLIII) and which thus remains *unreal* and *without object*. The difference between effective demand, supported by money, and ineffective demand, based upon my need, my passion, my desire, etc. is the difference between *being* and *thought*, between the merely inner representation and the representation which exists outside myself as a *real object*.

If I have no money for travel I have no *need*—no real and self-realizing need—for travel. If I have a *vocation* for study but no money for it, then I have *no* vocation, i.e. no *effective*, genuine vocation. Conversely, if I really have *no* vocation

---

[1] Marx omitted a word here in the manuscript. [*Editor's note.*]

for study, but have money and the urge for it, then I have an *effective* vocation. *Money* is the external, universal means and power (not derived from man as man nor from human society as society) to change *representation* into *reality* and *reality* into *mere representation*. It transforms *real human and natural faculties* into mere abstract representations, i.e. *imperfections* and tormenting chimeras; and on the other hand, it transforms *real imperfections and fancies*, faculties which are really impotent and which exist only in the individual's imagination, into *real faculties and powers*. In this respect, therefore, money is the general inversion of *individualities*, turning them into their opposites and associating contradictory qualities with their qualities.

Money, then, appears as a *disruptive* power for the individual and for the social bonds, which claim to be self-subsistent *entities*. It changes fidelity into infidelity, love into hate, hate into love, virtue into vice, vice into virtue, servant into master, stupidity into intelligence and intelligence into stupidity.

Since money, as the existing and active concept of value, confounds and exchanges everything, it is the universal *confusion and transposition* of all things, the inverted world, the confusion and transposition of all natural and human qualities.

He who can purchase bravery is brave, though a coward. Money is not exchanged for a particular quality, a particular thing, or a specific human faculty, but for the whole objective world of man and nature. Thus, from the standpoint of its possessor, it exchanges every quality and object for every other, even though they are contradictory. It is the fraternization of incompatibles; it forces contraries to embrace.

Let us assume *man* to be *man*, and his relation to the world to be a human one. Then love can only be exchanged for love, trust for trust, etc. If you wish to enjoy art you must be an artistically cultivated person; if you wish to influence other people you must be a person who really has a stimulating and encouraging effect upon others. Every one of your relations to man and to nature must be a *specific expression*, corresponding to the object of your will, of your *real individual* life. If you love without evoking love in return, i.e. if you are not able, by the *manifestation* of yourself as a loving person, to make yourself a *beloved person*, then your love is impotent and a misfortune.

CRITIQUE OF HEGEL'S DIALECTIC AND
GENERAL PHILOSOPHY

THIS is perhaps an appropriate point at which to explain and substantiate what has been said, and to make some general comments upon Hegel's dialectic, especially as it is expounded in the *Phenomenology* and *Logic*, and upon its relation to the modern critical movement.

Modern German criticism was so much concerned with the past, and was so hampered by its involvement with its subject-matter, that it had a wholly uncritical attitude to the methods of criticism and completely ignored the partly formal, but in fact *essential* question—how do we now stand with regard to the Hegelian *dialectic*? This ignorance of the relationship of modern criticism to Hegel's general philosophy and his dialectic in particular was so great that critics such as Strauss and Bruno Bauer (the former in all his writings; the latter in his *Synoptiker*,[1] where, in opposition to Strauss, he substitutes the " self-consciousness " of abstract man for the substance of " abstract nature," and even in *Das entdeckte Christentum* [2]) were, at least implicity, ensnared in Hegelian logic. Thus, for instance, in *Das entdeckte Christentum* it is argued: " As if self-consciousness in positing the world, that which is different, did not produce itself in producing its object; for it then annuls the difference between itself and what it has produced, since it exists only in this creation and movement, has its purpose only in this movement, etc." [3] Or again: " They (the French

---

[1] BRUNO BAUER, *Kritik der evangelischen Geschichte des Johannes*, Bremen, 1840; *Kritik der evangelischen Geschichte der Synoptiker*, II Band, Leipzig, 1841; III Band, Braunschweig, 1842.

[2] Ibid., *Das entdeckte Christentum. Eine Erinnerung an das achtzehnte Jahrhundert und ein Beitrag zur Krisis des neunzehnten*, Zürich and Winterthur, 1843.

[3] Ibid., p. 113. Marx paraphrases the end of this passage. [*Editor's note.*]

materialists) could not see that the movement of the universe has only become real and unified in itself in so far as it is the movement of self-consciousness." [1]   These expressions not only do not differ from the Hegelian conception, but reproduce it textually.

[XLII] How little these writers, in undertaking their criticism (Bauer in his *Synoptiker*), were aware of their relation to Hegel's dialectic, and how little such an awareness emerged from the criticism, is demonstrated by Bauer in his *Gute Sache der Freiheit* [2] when, instead of replying to the indiscreet question put by Gruppe, " And now what is to be done with logic?", he transmits it to future critics.

Now that Feuerbach, in his " Thesen " in the *Anecdotis* [3] and in greater detail in his *Philosophie der Zukunft*,[4] has demolished the inner principle of the old dialectic and philosophy, the " Critical School," which was unable to do this itself but has seen it accomplished, has proclaimed itself the pure, decisive, absolute, and finally enlightened criticism, and in its spiritual pride has reduced the whole historical movement to the relation existing between itself and the rest of the world, which comes into the category of " the mass." It has reduced all dogmatic antitheses to the single dogmatic antithesis between its own cleverness and the stupidity of the world, between the critical Christ and mankind—" the rabble." [5]   At every moment of the day it has demonstrated its own excellence *vis-à-vis* the stupidity of the mass, and it has finally announced the critical *last judgement* by proclaim-

---

[1] Op. cit., p. 114.

[2] BRUNO BAUER, *Die gute Sache der Freiheit und meine eigene Angelegenheit*, Zürich and Winterthur, 1842, p. 193.   Bauer's reference is to Marheinecke, not Gruppe.   [*Editor's note.*]

[3] ARNOLD RUGE (Ed.), *Anekdota zur neuesten deutschen Philosophie und Publizistik*, Zürich and Winterthur, 1843, Band II, p. 62 *et seq.*   " Vorläufige Thesen zur Reformation der Philosophie " von Ludwig Feuerbach.

[4] LUDWIG FEUERBACH, *Grundsätze der Philosophie der Zukunft*, Zürich and Witherthur, 1843.

[5] *See*, for example, *Allgemeine Literatur-Zeitung Monatsschrift*, edited by Bruno Bauer, Band I–II.   Charlottenburg, 1844; no. 1, p. 1 *et seq.*, no. 5, p. 23 *et seq.*, no. 8, p. 18 *et seq.*   [*Editor's note.*]

ing that the day is at hand when the whole of fallen mankind will assemble before it and will be divided up into groups each of which will be handed its *testimonium paupertatis* (certificate of poverty).[1] The Critical School has made public its superiority to all human feelings and to the world, above which it sits enthroned in sublime solitude, content to utter occasionally from its sarcastic lips the laughter of the Olympian gods. After all these entertaining antics of idealism (of Young Hegelianism) which is expiring in the form of criticism, the Critical School has not even now intimated that it was necessary to discuss critically its own source, the dialectic of Hegel; nor has it given any indication of its relation with the dialectic of Feuerbach. This is a procedure totally lacking in critical sense.

Feuerbach is the only person who has a *serious* and *critical* relation to Hegel's dialectic, who has made real discoveries in this field, and above all, who has vanquished the old philosophy. The magnitude of Feuerbach's achievement and the unassuming simplicity with which he presents his work to the world are in striking contrast with the behaviour of others.

Feuerbach's great achievement is—

1. to have shown that philosophy is nothing more than religion brought into thought and developed by thought, and that it is equally to be condemned as another form and mode of existence of human alienation;

2. to have founded *genuine materialism* and *positive science* by making the social relationship of " man to man " the basic principle of his theory;

3. to have opposed to the negation of the negation which claims to be the absolute positive, a self-subsistent principle positively founded on itself.

Feuerbach explains Hegel's dialectic, and at the same time justifies taking the positive phenomenon, that which is

[1] *Allgemeine Literatur-Zeitung Monatsschrift*, no. 5, p. 15.

perceptible and indubitable, as the starting-point, in the following way.

Hegel begins from the alienation of substance (logically, from the infinite, the abstract universal) from the absolute and fixed abstraction; i.e. in ordinary language, from religion and theology. Secondly, he supersedes the infinite, and posits the real, the perceptible, the finite, and the particular. (Philosophy, supersession of religion and theology.) Thirdly, he then supersedes the positive and re-establishes the abstraction, the infinite. (Re-establishment of religion and theology.)

Thus Feuerbach conceives the negation of the negation as being *only* a contradiction within philosophy itself, which affirms theology (transcendence, etc.) after having superseded it, and thus affirms it in opposition to philosophy.

For the positing or self-affirmation and self-confirmation which is implied in the negation of the negation is regarded as a positing which is still uncertain, burdened with its contrary, doubtful of itself and thus incomplete, not demonstrated by its own existence, and implicit. [XIII] The positing which is perceptually indubitable and grounded upon itself is directly opposed to it.

In conceiving the negation of the negation, from the aspect of the positive relation inherent in it, as the only true positive, and from the aspect of the negative relation inherent in it, as the only true act and the self-confirming act of all being, Hegel has merely discovered an *abstract, logical* and *speculative* expression of the historical process, which is not yet the *real* history of man as a given subject, but only the history of the *act of creation*, of the *genesis of man*.

We shall explain both the abstract form of this process and the difference between the process as conceived by Hegel and by modern criticism, by Feuerbach in *Das Wesen des Christentums*; or rather, the critical form of this process which is still so uncritical in Hegel.

Let us examine Hegel's system. It is necessary to begin

with the *Phenomenology*,[1] because it is there that Hegel's philosophy was born and that its secret is to be found.

Phenomenology

A. *Self-consciousness*

I. *Consciousness.* (α) Certainty in sense experience, or the " this " and meaning. (β) Perception, or the thing with its properties, and illusion. (γ) Power and understanding, phenomena and the supersensible world.

II. *Self-consciousness.* The truth of certainty of oneself. (*a*) Independence and dependence of self-consciousness, domination and servitude. (*b*) Freedom of self-consciousness. Stoicism, scepticism, the unhappy consciousness.

III. *Reason.* Certainty and truth of reason. (*a*) Observational reason: observation of nature and of self-consciousness. (*b*) Self-realization of the rational self-consciousness. Pleasure and necessity. The law of the heart and the frenzy of vanity. Virtue and the way of the world. (*c*) Individuality which is real in and for itself. Legislative reason. Reason which tests laws.

B. *Spirit*

I. True spirit; customary morality.
II. Self-alienated spirit; culture.
III. Spirit certain of itself; morality.

C. *Religion*

Natural religion, the religion of art, revealed religion.

D. *Absolute knowledge* [2]

Hegel's *Encyclopaedia* [3] begins with logic, with *pure speculative thought*, and ends with *absolute knowledge*, the self-conscious

---

[1] G. W. F. HEGEL, *System der Wissenschaft, Erster Teil: Die Phänomenologie des Geistes,* Bamberg and Würzburg, 1807.

[2] These are the chapter and section headings of Hegel's *Phenomenology of Spirit.* [*Editor's note.*]

[3] G. W. F. HEGEL, *Encyclopädie der philosophischen Wissenschaften im Grundrisse.*

and self-conceiving philosophical or absolute mind, i.e. the superhuman, abstract mind. The whole of the *Encyclopaedia* is nothing but the extended being of the philosophical mind, its self-objectification; and the philosophical mind is nothing but the alienated world-mind thinking within the bounds of its self-alienation, i.e. conceiving itself in an abstract manner. *Logic* is the *money* of the mind, the speculative *thought-value* of man and of nature, their essence indifferent to any real determinate character and thus unreal; *thought* which is *alienated* and abstract and ignores real nature and man. *The external character of this abstract thought* . . . *nature* as it exists for this abstract thought. Nature is external to it, loss of itself, and is only conceived as something external, as abstract thought, but alienated abstract thought. Finally, spirit, this thought which returns to its own origin and which, as anthropological, phenomenological, psychological, customary, artistic-religious spirit, is not valid for itself until it discovers itself and relates itself to itself as absolute knowledge in the absolute (i.e. abstract) spirit, and so receives its conscious and fitting existence. For its real mode of existence is *abstraction*.

Hegel commits a double error. The first appears most clearly in the *Phenomenology*, the birthplace of his philosophy. When Hegel conceives wealth, the power of the state, etc. as entities alienated from the human being, he conceives them only in their thought form. They are entities of thought and thus simply an alienation of *pure* (i.e. abstract) philosophical thought. The whole movement, therefore, ends in absolute knowledge. It is precisely abstract thought from which these objects are alienated, and which they confront with their presumptuous reality. The *philosopher*, himself an abstract form of alienated man, sets himself up as the *measure* of the alienated world. The whole *history of alienation*, and of the retraction of alienation, is, therefore, only the *history of the production* of abstract thought, i.e. of absolute, logical, speculative thought. *Estrangement*, which thus forms the real interest of this alienation and of the supersession of this alienation, is the opposition of *in itself* and *for itself*, of *consciousness* and *self-consciousness*, of *object* and *subject*, i.e. the opposition in thought itself between abstract thought and sensible reality or real sensuous existence. All other contradictions and movements are merely the *appearance*, the *cloak*, the *exoteric* form of these two opposites which are alone important and which constitute the *significance* of the other, profane contradictions. It is not the fact that the human being *objectifies* himself *inhumanly*, in opposition to himself, but that he *objectifies* himself by *distinction* from and in *opposition* to abstract thought, which constitutes alienation as it exists and as it has to be transcended.

[XVIII] The appropriation of man's objectified and alienated faculties is thus, in the first place, only an *appropriation* which occurs in *consciousness*, in *pure thought*, i.e. in abstraction. It is the appropriation of these objects as *thoughts* and as *movements of thought*. For this reason, despite its thoroughly negative and critical appearance, and despite the genuine criticism which it contains and which often anticipates later developments, there is already implicit in the *Phenomenology*, as a germ, as a potentiality and a secret, the uncritical positivism and uncritical idealism of Hegel's later works—the philosophical dissolution and restoration of the existing empirical world. *Secondly*, the vindication of the objective world for man (for example, the recognition that *sense* perception is not *abstract* sense perception but *human* sense perception, that religion, wealth, etc. are only the alienated reality of *human* objectification, of *human* faculties put to work, and are, therefore, a *way* to genuine *human* reality), this appropriation, or the insight into this process, appears in Hegel as the recognition of *sensuousness*, *religion*, state power, etc. as *mental* phenomena, for *mind* alone is the *true* essence of man, and the true form of mind is thinking mind, the logical, speculative mind. The *human character* of nature, of historically produced nature, of man's products, is shown by their being *products* of abstract mind, and thus phases of *mind, entities of thought.* The *Phenomenology* is a concealed, unclear and mystifying criticism, but in so far as it grasps the *alienation* of man (even though man appears only as mind) *all* the elements of criticism are contained in it, and are often *presented* and *worked out* in a manner which goes far beyond Hegel's own point of view. The sections devoted to the " unhappy consciousness," the " honest consciousness," the struggle between the " noble " and the " base " consciousness, etc., etc. contain the *critical* elements (though still in an alienated form) of whole areas such as religion, the state, civil life, etc. Just as the *entity*, the *object*, appears as an entity of thought, so also the *subject* is always *consciousness* or *self-consciousness*; or rather, the object appears only as *abstract* consciousness and man as *self-consciousness.* Thus the distinctive forms of alienation which are manifested are only different forms of consciousness and self-consciousness. Since abstract consciousness (the form in which the object is conceived) is in *itself* merely a distinctive moment of self-consciousness, the outcome of the movement is the identity of self-consciousness and consciousness—absolute knowledge— the movement of abstract thought not directed outwards but proceeding within itself; i.e. the dialectic of pure thought is the result.

[XXIII] The outstanding achievement of Hegel's *Phenomenology*—the dialectic of negativity as the moving and creating principle—is, first, that Hegel grasps the self-creation of man as a process, objectification as loss of the object, as alienation and transcendence of this alienation, and that he, therefore, grasps the nature of *labour*, and conceives objective man (true, because real man) as the result of his *own labour.* The *real*, active orientation of man to himself as a species-being, or the affirmation of himself as a real species-being (i.e. as a human being) is only possible so far as he really brings forth all his *species-powers* (which is only possible through the co-operative endeavours of mankind and as an outcome of history) and treats these powers as objects, which can only be done at first in the form of alienation.

We shall next show in detail Hegel's one-sidedness and limitations, as revealed in the final chapter of the *Phenomenology*, on absolute knowledge; a chapter which contains the concentrated spirit of the *Phenomenology*, its relation to the dialectic, and also Hegel's *consciousness* of both and of their interrelations.

For the present, let us make these preliminary observations: Hegel's standpoint is that of modern political economy. He conceives *labour* as the *essence*, the self-confirming essence of man; he observes only the positive side of labour, not its negative side. Labour is *man's coming to be for himself* within *alienation*, or as an *alienated* man. Labour as Hegel understands and recognizes it is *abstract mental* labour. Thus, that which above all constitutes the *essence* of philosophy, the *alienation of man knowing himself*, or *alienated* science *thinking* itself, Hegel grasps as its essence. Consequently, he is able to bring together the separate elements of earlier philosophy and to present his own as the philosophy. What other philosophers did, that is, to conceive separate elements of nature and of human life as phases of self-consciousness and indeed of abstract self-consciousness, Hegel *knows* by *doing* philosophy; therefore, his science is absolute.

Let us now turn to our subject.

Absolute knowledge. The final chapter of the " Phenomenology."

The main point is that the *object of consciousness* is nothing else but *self-consciousness*, that the object is only *objectified* self-consciousness, self-consciousness as an object. (Positing man = self-consciousness.)

It is necessary, therefore, to surmount the *object of consciousness*. *Objectivity* as such is regarded as an alienated human relationship which does not correspond with the *essence of man*, self-consciousness. The reappropriation of the objective essence of man, which was produced as something alien and determined by alienation, signifies the super-session not only of *alienation* but also of *objectivity*; that is, man is regarded as a *non-objective, spiritual* being.

The process of *overcoming the object of consciousness* is described by Hegel as follows: The *object* does not reveal itself only as *returning* into the Self (according to Hegel that is a *one-sided* conception of the movement, considering only one aspect). Man is equated with self. The Self, however, is only man conceived *abstractly* and produced by abstraction. Man is self-referring. His eye, his ear, etc. are *self-referring*; every one of his faculties has this quality of *self*-reference. But it is entirely false to say on that account, " *Self-consciousness* has eyes, ears, faculties." Self-consciousness is rather a quality of human nature, of the human eye, etc.; human nature is not a quality of [XXIV] *self-consciousness*.

The Self, abstracted and determined for itself, is man as an *abstract egoist*, purely abstract *egoism* raised to the level of thought. (We shall return to this point later.)

For Hegel, *human life, man*, is equivalent to *self-consciousness*. All alienation of human life is, therefore, *nothing* but *alienation of self-consciousness*. The alienation of self-consciousness is not regarded as the *expression*, reflected in knowledge and thought, of the *real* alienation of human life. Instead, *actual* alienation, that which appears real, is in its *innermost* hidden nature (which philosophy first discloses) only the *phenomenal being* of the alienation of real human life, of *self-consciousness*. The science which comprehends this is therefore called *Phenomenology*. All reappropriation of alienated objective life appears, therefore, as an incorporation in self-consciousness. The person who takes possession of his being is only the self-consciousness which takes possession of objective being; the return of the object into the Self is, therefore, the reappropriation of the object.

Expressed in a *more comprehensive way* the *supersession of the object of consciousness* means: (1) that the object as such presents itself to consciousness as something disappearing;

(2) that it is the alienation of self-consciousness which establishes " thinghood "; (3) that this alienation has *positive* as well as *negative* significance; (4) that it has this significance not only *for us* or in itself, but also *for self-consciousness itself*; (5) that for *self-consciousness* the negative of the object, its self-supersession, has *positive* significance, or self-consciousness *knows* thereby the nullity of the object in that self-consciousness alienates itself, for in this alienation it establishes *itself* as object or, for the sake of the indivisible unity of *being-for-itself*, establishes the object as itself; (6) that, on the other hand, this other " moment " is equally present, that self-consciousness has superseded and reabsorbed this alienation and objectivity, and is thus *at home* in its other being as such; (7) that this is the movement of consciousness, and consciousness is, therefore, the totality of its " moments "; (8) that similarly, consciousness must have related itself to the object in all its determinations, and have conceived it in terms of each of them. This totality of determinations makes the object *intrinsically* a *spiritual being*, and it becomes truly so for consciousness by the apprehension of every one of these determinations as the Self, or by what was called earlier the *spiritual* attitude towards them.

ad (1) That the object as such presents itself to consciousness as something disappearing is the above-mentioned *return of the object into the Self*.

ad (2) *The alienation of self-consciousness* establishes " thinghood." Because man equals self-consciousness, his alienated objective being or " *thinghood* " is equivalent to *alienated self-consciousness*, and " thinghood " is established by this alienation. (" Thinghood " is that which is *an object for him*, and an object for him is really only that which is an essential object, consequently his *objective* essence. And since it is not the *real man*, nor *nature*—man being *human nature*—who becomes as such a subject, but only an abstraction of man, self-consciousness, " thinghood " can only be *alienated self-consciousness*.) It is quite understandable that a living, natural being endowed with objective (i.e. material) faculties should have *real natural objects* of its being, and equally that its self-alienation should be the establishment of a *real*, objective world, but in the form of *externality*, as a world which does not belong to, and dominates, its being. There is nothing incomprehensible or mysterious about this. The converse, rather, would be mysterious. But it is equally clear that a self-consciousness, i.e. its alienation, can only establish " *thinghood*," i.e. only an abstract thing, a thing created by abstraction and not a real thing. It is [XXVI] clear, moreover, that " thinghood " is totally lacking in *independence*, in *being*, *vis-à-vis* self-consciousness; it is a mere *construct* established by self-consciousness. And what is established is not self-confirming; it is the confirmation of the act of establishing, which for an instant, but only for an instant, fixes its energy as a product and *apparently* confers upon it the role of an independent, real being.

When real, corporeal *man*, with his feet firmly planted on the solid ground, inhaling and exhaling all the powers of nature, *posits* his real objective faculties, as a result of his alienation, as alien objects, the *positing* is not the subject of this act but the subjectivity of *objective* faculties whose action must also, therefore, be *objective*. An objective being acts objectively, and it would not act objectively if objectivity were not part of its essential being. It creates and establishes *only objects*, *because* it is established by objects, and because it is fundamentally *natural*. In the act of establishing it does not descend from its " pure activity " to the *creation of objects*; its *objective* product simply confirms its *objective* activity, its activity as an objective, natural being.

We see here how consistent naturalism or humanism is distinguished from both idealism and materialism, and at the same time constitutes their unifying truth. We see also that only naturalism is able to comprehend the process of world history.

Man is directly a *natural being*. As a natural being, and as a living natural being he is, on the one hand, endowed with *natural powers* and *faculties*, which exist in him as tendencies and abilities, as *drives*. On the other hand, as a natural, embodied, sentient, objective being he is a *suffering*, conditioned and limited being, like animals and plants. The *objects* of his drives exist outside himself as *objects* independent of him, yet they are *objects* of his *needs*, essential *objects* which are indispensable to the exercise and confirmation of his faculties. The fact that man is an *embodied*, living, real, sentient, objective being with natural powers, means that he has *real*, *sensuous objects* as the objects of his being, or that he can only express his being in real, sensuous objects. *To be* objective, natural, sentient and at the same time to have object, nature and sense outside oneself, or to be oneself object, nature and sense for a third person, is the same thing. *Hunger* is a natural *need*; it requires, therefore, a *nature* outside itself, an *object* outside itself, in order to be satisfied and stilled. Hunger is the objective need of a body for an *object* which exists outside itself and which is essential for its integration and the expression of its nature. The sun is an *object*, a necessary and life-assuring object, for the plant, just as the plant is an object for the sun, an *expression* of the sun's life-giving power and *objective* essential powers.

A being which does not have its nature outside itself is not a *natural* being and does not share in the being of nature. A being which has no object outside itself is not an objective being. A being which is not itself an object for a third being has no being for its *object*, i.e. it is not objectively related and its being is not objective.

[XXVII] A non-objective being is a *non-being*. Suppose a being which neither is an object itself nor has an object. In the first place, such a being would be the *only* being; no other being would exist outside itself and it would be solitary and alone. For as soon as there exist objects outside myself, as soon as I am not *alone*, I am *another*, *another reality* from the object outside me. For this third object I am thus an *other reality* than itself, i.e. *its object.* To suppose a being which is not the object of another being would be to suppose that *no* objective being exists. As soon as I have an object, this object has me for its object. But a *non-objective* being is an unreal, non-sensuous, merely conceived being; i.e. a merely imagined being, an abstraction. To be *sensuous,* i.e. real, is to be an object of sense or *sensuous* object, and thus to have sensuous objects outside oneself, objects of one's sensations. To be sentient is to *suffer* (to experience).

Man as an objective sentient being is a *suffering* being, and since he feels his suffering, a *passionate* being. Passion is man's faculties striving to attain their object.

But man is not merely a natural being; he is a *human* natural being. He is a being for himself, and, therefore, a *species-being;* and as such he has to express and authenticate himself in being as well as in thought. Consequently, *human* objects are not natural objects as they present themselves directly, nor is *human sense,* as it is immediately and objectively *given,* *human* sensibility and human objectivity. Neither objective nature nor subjective nature is directly presented in a form adequate to the *human* being. And as everything natural must have its *origin* so *man* has his process of genesis, *history,* which is for him, however, a conscious process and thus one which is consciously self-transcending. (We shall return to this point later.)

Thirdly, since this establishment of " thinghood " is itself only an appearance, an act which contradicts the nature of pure activity, it has to be annulled again and " thinghood " has to be denied.

ad 3, 4, 5, 6. (3) This alienation of consciousness has not only a negative but also a positive significance, and (4) it has this positive significance not only *for us* or in itself, but for consciousness itself. (5) For *consciousness* the negation of the object, or its annulling of itself by that means, has positive significance; it *knows* the nullity of the object by the fact that it alienates *itself,* for in this alienation it *knows* itself as the object or, for the sake of the indivisible unit of *being-for self*, knows the object as itself. (6) On the other hand, this other " moment " is equally present, but consciousness has superseded and reabsorbed this alienation and objectivity and is thus *at home in its other being as such*.

We have already seen that the appropriation of alienated objective being, or the supersession of objectivity in the form of *alienation* (which has to develop from indifferent otherness to real antagonistic alienation), signifies for Hegel also, or primarily, the supersession of *objectivity*, since it is not the determinate character of the object but its *objective* character which is the scandal of alienation for self-consciousness. The object is therefore negative, self-annulling, a *nullity*. This nullity of the object has a positive significance because it *knows* this nullity, objective being, as its *self-alienation*, and knows that this nullity exists only through its self-alienation. . . .

The way in which consciousness is, and in which something is for it, is *knowing*. Knowing is its only act. Thus something comes to exist for consciousness so far as it *knows* this *something*. Knowing is its only objective relation. It knows, then, the nullity of the object (i.e. knows the non-existence of the distinction between itself and the object, the non-existence of the object for it) because it knows the object as its *self-alienation*. That is to say, it knows itself (knows knowing as an object), because the object is only the *semblance* of an object, a deception, which is intrinsically nothing but knowing itself which has confronted itself with itself, has established in face of itself a *nullity*, a " something " which has *no* objective existence outside the knowing itself. Knowing knows that in relating itself to an object it is only *outside* itself, alienates itself, and that *it* only *appears* to itself as an object; or in other words, that that which appears to it as an object is only itself.

On the other hand, Hegel says, this other " moment " is present at the same time; namely, that consciousness has equally superseded and reabsorbed this alienation and objectivity, and consequently is *at home in its other being as such*.

In this discussion all the illusions of speculation are assembled.

First, consciousness—self-consciousness—is *at home in its other being as such*. It is, therefore—if we abstract from Hegel's abstraction and substitute the self-consciousness of man for self-consciousness—*at home in its other being as such*. This implies, first, that consciousness (knowing as knowing, thinking as thinking) claims to be directly the *other* of itself, the sensuous world, reality, life; it is thought over-reaching itself in thought (Feuerbach). This aspect is contained in it, in so far as consciousness as mere consciousness is offended not by the alienated objectivity but by *objectivity as such*.

Secondly, it implies that self-conscious man, in so far as he has recognized and superseded the spiritual world (or the universal spiritual mode of existence of his world) then confirms it again in this alienated form and presents it as his true existence; he re-establishes it and claims to *be at home in his other being*. Thus, for example, after superseding religion, when he has recognized religion as a product of self-alienation, he then finds a confirmation of himself in *religion as religion*. *This is* the root of Hegel's *false* positivism, or of his merely *apparent* criticism; what Feuerbach calls the positing, negation and re-establishment of religion or theology, but which has to be conceived in a more general way. Thus reason is at home in unreason as such. Man, who has recognized that he leads an alienated life in law, politics, etc. leads his true human life in this alienated life as such. Self-affirmation, in contradiction with itself, with the knowledge and the nature of the object, is thus the true *knowledge* and *life*.

There can no longer be any question about Hegel's compromise with religion, the state, etc., for this falsehood is the falsehood of his whole argument.

[XXIX] If I *know* religion as *alienated* human self-consciousness what I know in it as religion is not my self-consciousness but my alienated self-consciousness confirmed in it. Thus my own self, and the self-consciousness which is its essence, is not confirmed in *religion* but in the *abolition* and *supersession* of religion.

In Hegel, therefore, the negation of the negation is not the confirmation of true being by the negation of illusory being. It is the confirmation of illusory being, or of self-alienating being in its denial; or the denial of this illusory being as an objective being existing outside man and independently of him, and its transformation into a subject.

The act of *supersession* plays a strange part in which *denial* and preservation, denial and affirmation, are linked together. Thus, for example, in Hegel's *Philosophy of Right*, *private right* superseded equals *morality*, morality superseded equals *the family*, the family superseded equals *civil society*, civil society superseded equals the *state*, and the state superseded equals *world history*. But in *actuality* private right, morality, the family, civil society, the state, etc. remain; only they have become " moments," modes of existence of man, which have no validity in isolation but which mutually dissolve and engender one another. *They are " moments " of the movement*.

In their actual existence this *mobile* nature is concealed. It is first revealed in thought, in philosophy; consequently, my true religious existence is my existence in the *philosophy of religion*, my true political existence is my existence in the *philosophy of right*, my true natural existence is my existence in the *philosophy of nature*, my true artistic existence is my existence in the *philosophy of art*, and my true human existence is my existence in *philosophy*. In the same way, the true existence of religion, the state, nature and art, is the *philosophy* of religion, of the state, of nature, and of art. But if the philosophy of religion is the only true existence of religion I am only truly religious as a *philosopher of religion*, and I deny *actual* religious sentiment and the actual *religious* man. At the same time, however, I *confirm* them, partly in my own existence or in the alien existence with which I confront them (for this *is* only their philosophical expression), and partly in their own original form, since they are for me the merely *apparent* other being, allegories, the lineaments of their own true existence (i.e. of my *philosophical* existence) concealed by sensuous draperies.

In the same way, *quality* superseded equals *quantity*, quantity superseded equals *measure*, measure superseded equals *being*, being superseded equals *phenomenal being*, phenomenal being superseded equals *actuality*, actuality superseded equals the *concept*, the concept superseded equals *objectivity*, objectivity superseded equals the *absolute idea*, the absolute idea superseded equals *nature*, nature superseded equals *subjective* spirit, subjective spirit superseded equals *ethical* objective spirit, *ethical* spirit superseded equals *art*, art superseded equals *religion*, and religion superseded equals *absolute knowledge*.

On the other hand, this supersession is supersession of an entity of thought; thus, private property *as thought* is superseded in the *thought* of morality.   And since thought imagines itself to be, without mediation, the other aspect of itself, namely *sensuous reality*, and takes its own action for *real, sensuous action*, this supersession in thought, which leaves its object in existence in the real world, believes itself to have really overcome it.   On the other hand, since the object has now become for it a " moment " of thought, it is regarded in its real existence as a confirmation of thought, of self-consciousness, of abstraction.

[XXX] From the one aspect the existent which Hegel *supersedes* in philosophy is not therefore the *actual* religion, state or nature, but religion itself as an object of knowledge, i.e. *dogmatics*; and similarly with *jurisprudence, political science* and *natural science*.   From this aspect, therefore, he stands in opposition both to the actual being and to the direct, non-philosophical science (or the non-philosophical *concepts*) of this being. Thus he contradicts the conventional conceptions.

From the other aspect, the religious man, etc. can find in Hegel his ultimate confirmation.

We have now to consider the *positive* moments of Hegel's dialectic, within the condition of alienation.

(*a*) *Supersession* as an objective movement which *reabsorbs* alienation into itself. This is the insight, expressed within alienation, into the *appropriation* of the objective being through the supersession of its alienation. It is the alienated insight into the *real objectification* of man, into the real appropriation of his objective being by the destruction of the *alienated* character of the objective world, by the annulment of its alienated mode of existence. In the same way, atheism as the annulment of God is the emergence of theoretical humanism, and communism as the annulment of private property is the vindication of real human life as man's property. The latter is also the emergence of practical humanism, for atheism is humanism mediated to itself by the annulment of religion, while communism is humanism mediated to itself by the annulment of private property. It is only by the supersession of this mediation (which is, however, a necessary pre-condition) that the self-originating *positive* humanism can appear.

But atheism and communism are not flight or abstraction from, nor loss of, the objective world which men have created by the objectification of their faculties. They are not an impoverished return to unnatural, primitive simplicity. They are rather the first real emergence, the genuine actualization, of man's nature as something real.

Thus Hegel, in so far as he sees the *positive* significance of the self-referring negation (though in an alienated mode) conceives man's self-estrangement, alienation of being, loss of objectivity and reality, as self-discovery, change of nature, objectification and realization. In short, Hegel conceives labour as man's *act of self-creation* (though in abstract terms);

he grasps man's relation to himself as an alien being and the emergence of *species-consciousness* and *species-life* as the demonstration of his alien being.

(*b*) But in Hegel, apart from, or rather as a consequence of, the inversion we have already described, this act of genesis appears, in the first place, as one which is merely *formal*, because it is abstract, and because human nature itself is treated as merely *abstract, thinking nature*, as self-consciousness.

Secondly, because the conception is *formal* and *abstract* the annulment of alienation becomes a confirmation of alienation. For Hegel, this movement of *self-creation* and *self-objectification* in the form of *self-estrangement* is the *absolute* and hence final *expression of human life*, which has its end in itself, is at peace with itself and at one with its own nature.

This movement, in its abstract [XXXI] form as dialectic, is regarded therefore as *truly human life*, and since it is nevertheless an abstraction, an alienation of human life, it is regarded as a *divine process* and thus as the divine process of mankind; it is a process which man's abstract, pure, absolute being, as distinguished from himself, traverses.

Thirdly, this process must have a bearer, a subject; but the subject first emerges as a result. This result, the subject knowing itself as absolute self-consciousness, is therefore *God, absolute spirit, the self-knowing and self-manifesting idea*. Real man and real nature become mere predicates, symbols of this concealed unreal man and unreal nature. Subject and predicate have, therefore, an inverted relation to each other; a *mystical subject-object*, or a *subjectivity reaching beyond the object*, the *absolute subject* as a process of self-alienation and of return from alienation into itself, and at the same time of reabsorption of this alienation, the *subject* as this process; pure, *unceasing* revolving within itself.

First, the formal and abstract conception of man's act of self-creation or self-objectification.

Since Hegel equates man with self-consciousness, the

alienated object, the alienated real being of man, is simply *consciousness*, merely the thought of alienation, its abstract and hence vacuous and unreal expression, the *negation*. The annulment of alienation is also, therefore, merely an abstract and vacuous annulment of this empty abstraction, the *negation of the negation*. The replete, living, sensuous, concrete activity of self-objectification is, therefore, reduced to a mere abstraction, *absolute negativity*, an abstraction which is then crystallized as such and is conceived as an independent activity, as activity itself. Since this so-called negativity is merely the *abstract, vacuous* form of that real living act, its content can only be a *formal* content produced by abstraction from all content. They are, therefore, general, abstract *forms of abstraction* which refer to any content and are thus neutral towards, and valid for, any content; forms of thought, logical forms which are detached from *real* spirit and *real* nature. (We shall expound later the *logical* content of absolute negativity.)

Hegel's positive achievement in his speculative logic is to show that the *determinate concepts*, the universal *fixed thought-forms*, in their independence from nature and spirit, are a necessary result of the general alienation of human nature and also of human thought; and to depict them as a whole as moments in the process of abstraction. For example, being superseded is essence, essence superseded is concept, the concept superseded is . . . the absolute idea. But what is the absolute idea? It must supersede itself if it does not want to traverse the whole process of abstraction again from the beginning and to rest content with being a totality of abstractions or a self-comprehending abstraction. But the self-comprehending abstraction knows itself to be nothing; it must abandon itself, the abstraction, and so arrives at an entity which is its exact opposite, *nature*. The whole *Logic* is therefore, a demonstration that abstract thought is nothing for itself, that the absolute idea is nothing for itself, that only *nature* is something.

[XXXII] The absolute idea, the *abstract* idea which " *regarded* from the aspect of its unity with itself, is *intuition* " (Hegel's *Encyclopaedia*, 3rd ed., p. 222), and which " in its own absolute truth *resolves* to let the moment of its particularity or of initial determination and other-being, the *immediate idea*, as its reflection, *emerge freely from itself as nature* " (ibid.); this whole idea which behaves in such a strange and fanciful way and which has given the Hegelians such terrible headaches is throughout nothing but *abstraction*, i.e. the abstract thinker. It is abstraction which, made wise by experience and enlightened about its own truth, resolves under various (false and still abstract) conditions to *abandon* itself, and to establish its other being, the particular, the determinate, in place of its self-absorption, non-being, universality and indeterminateness; and which resolves to let nature, which it concealed within itself only as an abstraction, as an entity of thought, *emerge freely from itself*. That is, it decides to forsake abstraction and to observe nature *free* from abstraction. The abstract idea, which without mediation becomes *intuition*, is nothing but abstract thought which abandons itself and decides for *intuition*. This whole transition from logic to the philosophy of nature is simply the transition from *abstracting* to *intuiting*, a transition which is extremely difficult for the abstract thinker to acomplish and which he therefore describes in such strange terms. The *mystical feeling* which drives the philosopher from abstract thinking to intuition is *ennui*, the longing for a content.

(Man alienated from himself is also the thinker alienated from his *being*, i.e. from his natural and human life. His thoughts are consequently spirits existing outside nature and man. In his *Logic* Hegel has imprisoned all these spirits together, and has conceived each of them first as negation, i.e. as *alienation of human* thought, and secondly as negation of the negation, i.e. as the supersession of this alienation and as the real expression of human thought. But since this negation of the negation is itself still confined within the alienation, it is in part a restoration of these fixed spiritual forms in their alienation, in part an immobilization in the final act, the act of self-reference, as the true being of these spiritual forms.[1] Further, in so far as this abstraction conceives itself, and experiences an increasing weariness of itself, there appears in Hegel an abandonment of abstract thought which moves solely in the sphere of thought, devoid of eyes, ears, teeth, everything, and a resolve to recognize *nature* as being and to go over to intuition.)

[XXXIII] But *nature* too, taken abstractly, for itself, and rigidly separated from man, is *nothing* for man. It goes without saying that the abstract thinker who has committed himself to intuition, intuits nature abstractly. As nature lay enclosed in the thinker in a form which was obscure and mysterious even to himself, as absolute idea, as an entity of thought, so in truth, when he let it emerge from himself it was still only *abstract nature*, nature as an *entity of thought*, but now with the significance that it is the other-being of thought, is real, intuited nature, distinguished from abstract thought. Or, to speak in human language, the abstract thinker discovers from intuiting nature that the entities which he thought to create out of nothing, out of pure abstraction, to create in the divine dialectic as the pure products of thought endlessly shuttling back and forth in itself and never regarding external reality, are simply *abstractions* from *natural characteristics*. The whole of nature, therefore, reiterates to him the logical abstractions, but in a sensuous, external form. He *analyses* nature and these abstractions again.

[1] That is, Hegel substitutes the act of abstraction revolving within itself, for these fixed abstractions. In so doing, he has first of all the merit of having indicated the source of all these inappropriate concepts which originally belonged to different philosophies, and of having brought them together and established the comprehensive range of abstractions, instead of some particular abstraction, as the object of criticism. We shall see later why Hegel separates thought from the *subject*. It is already clear, however, that if man is not human the expression of his nature cannot be human, and consequently thought itself could not be conceived as an expression of man's nature, as the expression of a human and natural subject, with eyes, ears, etc. living in society, in the world, and in nature.

His intuition of nature is, therefore, simply the act of confirmation of his abstraction from the intuition of nature;
his conscious re-enactment of the process of generating his
abstraction.   Thus, for example, Time equals Negativity
which refers to itself (loc. cit., p. 238).   In the natural form,
superseded Movement as Matter corresponds to superseded
Becoming as Being.   In the *natural* form Light is *Reflection-in-
itself*.   Body as *Moon* and *Comet* is the natural form of the
antithesis which, according to the *Logic*, is on the one hand
the *positive grounded upon itself*, and on the other hand, the
negative grounded upon itself.   The Earth is the *natural* form of
the logical *ground*, as the negative unity of the antithesis, etc.

Nature as nature, i.e. so far as it is sensuously distinguished
from that secret sense concealed within it, nature separated
and distinguished from these abstractions is *nothing* (a *nullity
demonstrating its nullity*), is *devoid of sense*, or has only the sense
of an external thing which has been superseded.

" In the finite-*teleological* view is to be found the correct
premise that nature does not contain within itself the
absolute purpose " (loc. cit., p. 225).   Its purpose is the
confirmation of abstraction.   " Nature has shown itself to
be the idea in the *form* of *other-being*.   Since the idea is in this
form the negative of itself, or *external to itself*, nature is not
just relatively external *vis-à-vis* this idea, but *externality* constitutes the form in which it exists as nature " (loc. cit.,
p. 227).

Externality should not be understood here as the *self-
externalizing world of sense*, open to the light and to man's
senses.   It has to be taken here in the sense of alienation, as
error, a defect, that which ought not to be.   For that which
is true is still the idea.   Nature is merely the form of its
other-being.   And since abstract thought is *being*, that which
is external to it is by its nature a merely *external thing*.   The
abstract thinker recognizes at the same time that *sensuousness,
externality* in contrast to thought which shuttles back and
forth *within itself*, is the essence of nature.   But at the same

time he expresses this antithesis is such a way that this *externality* of nature, and its *contrast* with thought, appears as a deficiency, and that nature distinguished from abstraction appears as a deficient being.   [XXXIV] A being which is deficient, not simply for me or in my eyes, but in itself, has something outside itself which it lacks.   That is to say, its being is something other than itself.   For the abstract thinker, nature must therefore supersede itself, because it is already posited by him as a potentially *superseded* being.

" *For us*, spirit has *nature as its premise*, being the *truth* of nature and thereby its *absolute primus*.   In this truth nature has *vanished*, and spirit has surrendered itself as the idea which has attained being-for-itself, whose *object*, as well as the *subject*, is the *concept*.   This identity is *absolute negativity*, for whereas in nature the concept has its perfect external objectivity, here its alienation has been superseded and the concept has become identical with itself.   It is this identity only so far as it is a return from nature " (loc. cit., p. 392).

" *Revelation*, as the *abstract* idea, is unmediated transition to, the *coming-to-be* of, nature; as the revelation of the spirit, which is free, it is the *establishment* of nature as *its own* world, an establishment which, as reflection, is simultaneously the *presupposition* of the world as independently existing nature. Revelation in conception is the creation of nature as spirit's own being, in which it acquires the *affirmation* and *truth* of its freedom."   " *The absolute is spirit*; this is the highest definition of the absolute."

AUTHORS AND WORKS CITED BY MARX

AESCHYLUS (525–456 B.C.)

ANACHARSIS (sixth century B.C.). Scythian philosopher; sometimes mentioned as one of the Seven Sages of Greece.

ARISTOTLE (384–322 B.C.)

BAUER, BRUNO (1809–82)
> *Kritik der evangelischen Geschichte der Synoptiker*, Vols. I–II (1841), III (1842).
> *Die gute Sache der Freiheit und meine eigene Angelegenheit* (1842).
> " Die Fähigkeit der heutigen Juden und Christen, frei zu werden," in *Einundzwanzig Bogen aus der Schweiz*, ed. Georg Herwegh (1843).
> *Die Judenfrage* (1843).
> *Das entdeckte Christentum* (1843).
> (ed.) *Allgemeine Literatur-Zeitung Monatsschrift*, Vols. I–II (1844).

BEAUMONT, GUSTAVE DE LA BONNINIÈRE DE (1802–66)
> *Marie, ou l'esclavage aux États-Unis* (1835).

BERGASSE, NICOLAS (1750–1832). French publicist; member of the National Assembly.

BUCHEZ, P. J. B. (1796–1865) and ROUX-LAVERGNE, P. C. (1802–94)
> *Histoire parlementaire de la Révolution française*, Vol. 28 (1836).

BURET, ANTOINE-EUGÈNE (1810–42)
> *De la misère des classes laborieuses en Angleterre et en France* (1840).

CABET, ETIENNE (1788–1856)

CHEVALIER, MICHEL (1806–79). French economist.

COURIER DE MÉRÉ, P. L. (1772–1825). French publicist.

DESMOULINS, CAMILLE (1760–94)
> *Révolutions de France et de Brabant* (Weekly journal, 1789–91).

DESTUTT DE TRACY, A. L. C. (1754–1836)
> *Eléments d'idéologie. Traité de la volonté et de ses effets* (2ème édition, 1818).

ENGELS, FRIEDRICH (1820–95)
> " Umrisse zu einer Kritik der Nationalökonomie " in *Deutsch-Französische Jahrbücher* (1843).

FEUERBACH, LUDWIG (1804–72)
> *Das Wesen des Christentums* (1841).
> " Vorläufige Thesen zur Reformation der Philosophie," in

Anekdota zur neuesten deutschen Philosophie und Publizistik, ed. A. Ruge (1843).
Grundsätze der Philosophie der Zukunft (1843).

FOURIER, CHARLES (1772–1837)

FUNKE, G. L. W.
Die aus der unbeschränkten Teilbarkeit des Grundeigentums hervorgehenden Nachteile (1839).

GANILH, CHARLES (1759–1836). French economist and politician.

GOETHE, J. W. VON (1749–1832)
Faust.

HALLER, K. L. VON (1768–1854). German official and publicist.

HAMILTON, THOMAS (1789–1842)
Men and Manners in America (1833).

HEGEL, G. W. F. (1770–1831)
Die Phänomenologie des Geistes (1807).
Wissenschaft der Logik (1812–16).
Encyklopädie der philosophischen Wissenschaften im Grundrisse (1817).
Grundlinien der Philosophie des Rechts (1821).

HERWEGH, GEORG (1817–75). German poet.
(ed.) *Einundzwanzig Bogen aus der Schweiz* (1843).

HESS, MOSES (1812–75)
" Sozialismus und Kommunismus," " Die eine und ganze Freiheit," and " Philosophie der Tat " in *Einundzwanzig Bogen aus der Schweiz* (1843).

KOSEGARTEN, WILHELM (1792–1868). German publicist.

LANCIZOLLE, K. W. VON DELEUZE DE (1796–1871). German historian of law.

LAUDERDALE, J. M., Earl of (1759–1839). Economist.

LEO, HEINRICH (1799–1878)
Studien und Skizzen zu einer Naturlehre des Staates (1833).

LOUDON, CHARLES (1801–44). Scottish medical writer.
Solution du problème de la population et de la subsistance, soumise à un médicin dans une série de lettres (1842).

LUTHER, MARTIN (1483–1546)

McCULLOCH, J. R. (1789–1864). Economist.

MALTHUS, T. R. (1766–1834)

MILL, JAMES (1773–1836)
Elements of Political Economy (1821).

MÖSER, JUSTUS (1720–94)
Patriotische Phantasien (1775–78).

MÜNZER, THOMAS (c. 1490–1525)
Hochverursachte Schutzrede und Antwort . . . (1524).

OWEN, ROBERT (1771–1858)

PECQUEUR, CONSTANTIN (1801–87)
Théorie nouvelle d'économie sociale et politique, ou études sur l'organisation des sociétés (1842).

PROUDHON, PIERRE-JOSEPH (1809–65)

QUESNAY, FRANÇOIS (1694–1774)

RICARDO, DAVID (1772–1823)
Principles of Political Economy and Taxation (1816). French edition, with notes and criticisms by J. B. Say (2ème édition, 1835).

ROUSSEAU, JEAN-JACQUES (1712–78)
Du contrat social, ou principes du droit politique (1762).

RUGE, ARNOLD (1802–80)
(ed.) *Anekdota zur neuesten deutschen Philosophie und Publizistik* (1843).
With Marx (ed.) *Deutsch-Französische Jahrbücher* (1844).

SAINT-SIMON, CLAUDE-HENRI, COMTE DE (1760–1825)

SAY, JEAN-BAPTISTE (1767–1832)
Traité d'économie politique (3ème édition, 1817).

SCHULZ, WILHELM (1797–1860)
Die Bewegung der Produktion. Eine geschichtlich-statistische Abhandlung (1843).

SHAKESPEARE, W. (1564–1616)
Timon of Athens.

SISMONDI, J. C. L. SIMONDE DE (1773–1842)
Nouveaux principes d'économie politique (1819).

SKARBEK, FRYDERYK (1792–1866)
Théorie des richesses sociales, suivie d'une bibliographie de l'économie politique (1829).

SMITH, ADAM (1723–90)
An Inquiry into the Nature and Causes of the Wealth of Nations (1776). French translation, with notes by G. Garnier (1802).

STRAUSS, DAVID FRIEDRICH (1808–74)
Das Leben Jesu (1835–36).

TOCQUEVILLE, A. C. H. CLÉREL DE (1805–59)
De la démocratie en Amérique (1835).

VILLEGARDELLE, FRANÇOIS (1810–56). French publicist; Fourierist; author of *Accord des intérêts dans l'association* (1844).

VINCKE, F. L. W. VON (1774–1844). German official and writer on public administration.

WEITLING, WILHELM (1808–71)

INDEX

Catalog

If you are interested in a list of fine Paperback
books, covering a wide range of subjects
and interests, send your name and address,
requesting your free catalog, to:

McGraw-Hill Paperbacks
330 West 42nd Street
New York, New York 10036